WINNING YOUR
DIVORCE
A Man's Survival Guide

WINNING YOUR
DIVORCE

A Man's Survival Guide

Timothy J. Horgan

A DUTTON BOOK

DUTTON
Published by the Penguin Group
Penguin Books USA Inc., 375 Hudson Street,
New York, New York 10014, U.S.A.
Penguin Books Ltd, 27 Wrights Lane,
London W8 5TZ, England
Penguin Books Australia Ltd, Ringwood,
Victoria, Australia
Penguin Books Canada Ltd, 10 Alcorn Avenue,
Toronto, Ontario, Canada M4V 3B2
Penguin Books (N.Z.) Ltd, 182–190 Wairau Road,
Auckland 10, New Zealand

Penguin Books Ltd, Registered Offices:
Harmondsworth, Middlesex, England

First published by Dutton, an imprint of Dutton Signet,
a division of Penguin Books USA Inc.
Distributed in Canada by McClelland & Stewart Inc.

First Printing, January, 1994
10 9 8 7 6 5 4 3 2 1

 REGISTERED TRADEMARK—MARCA REGISTRADA

LIBRARY OF CONGRESS CATALOGING-IN-PUBLICATION DATA:
Horgan, Timothy J.
    Winning your divorce : a man's survival guide / by Timothy J. Horgan.
        p. cm.
    ISBN 0-525-93761-7
    1. Divorce—Law and legislation—United States—Popular works. 2. Husbands—
United States—Manuals, handbooks, etc. I. Title.
KF535.Z9H66 1994
346.7301'66—dc20
[347.306166]   93-5938
                                                                                    CIP

Printed in the United States of America
Set in Century Expanded
Designed by Leonard Telesca

To Linda

Contents

CHAPTER **7**

Custody and Visitation 93

CHAPTER **8**

Alimony, Support, and the Separation Agreement 111

CHAPTER **9**

The Discovery Stage 129

CHAPTER **10**

Going to Trial 137

Acknowledgments

Whatever the weaknesses of this book, they would have been far greater without the kind help of friends and colleagues. Lawrence Graham, Esq., acted as cicerone in the beginning; Dick Woods of Fathers for Equal Rights and James Cook of the Joint Custody Association gave liberally of their resource files; and George Kehayas, Esq., always encouraged.

I am extremely grateful for the support of my literary agent, John L. Hochmann. Arnold Dolin has been a firm and patient editor, repeatedly prodding me to think of the general reader.

My family has provided a surfeit of light relief. The book is dedicated to my wife, to whom I owe everything.

Introduction: How the Pendulum Has Swung

Jack Smith was a devoted husband and father. He and Angela had been married for ten years and had two lovely children, both of whom were preschoolers. Jack was a medical technician and Angela a nurse. While they never seemed to have enough money, their lifestyle was comfortably middle class. They lived in an old Victorian house in a lovely suburb with a good school district; they owned two cars, one new and one old; and they always managed to afford a summer vacation away from home.

Jack was the quiet, gentle type, a man generally happy with his life and by choice the primary caregiver to his children. Angela was more the "driver" personality; she was discontented with their economic status and their social position in the community. Simply put, she wanted more out of life and made no secret of the fact. Their basic difference in personality meant that Jack and Angela had their share of arguments during the marriage, but Jack never worried about the underlying relationship—until the evening Angela informed him over dinner that she wanted a divorce.

Jack was stunned. In answer to his inevitable question "Why?" Angela simply replied that they were two different people on two different paths in life and it wasn't going to get any better. She wanted out—now!

They talked, argued, and outright fought for days, but Angela remained adamant. She was not interested in therapy or counseling. She simply wanted a divorce.

In the end Jack, as he had throughout his married life, succumbed to his wife's stronger personality. He moved out of the house at her request, and eventually found an inexpensive apartment in a less desirable neighborhood. When it came time to get a lawyer he naively retained the attorney who had handled their house closing. Angela, on the other hand, hired a "bomber" from a nearby major city who had the reputation of being expensive but worth every penny. She paid her lawyer's initial retainer out of their joint checking account.

When the smoke cleared, Angela ended up with the house, custody of the two children, and 78 percent of Jack's income in alimony and child support. Jack was also forced to pay for her attorney. Angela soon married a doctor with whom she had been having an affair during the last year of her marriage. Jack was left to live a diminished life, divorced not only from his wife but also from his children, his neighbors, and the community activities that had meant so much to him. He was also left with megadoses of anger, guilt, and personal failure.

Jack exists. He came to me as a client years later when his support payments had become overwhelming. I wasn't surprised by his story. In my practice as a matrimonial attorney representing both husbands and wives, I had met many Jacks, all victims of a divorce system that is out of control.

Popular mythology and the feminist movement contend

that the American legal system favors males. Nothing could be further from the truth. Consider the following:

- Why is it that the wife almost invariably gets the house and custody of the children?
- Why is it so difficult for men to obtain liberal visitation rights to see their children?
- Why does a husband often have to vacate his house, even if he is not to blame for the breakup?
- Why does a divorced father have little or no voice in how his children are raised?
- Why does the father have no control over how his child support money is spent?
- Why does the system seem to work on the automatic assumption that the man is the bad guy?

In a popular culture that focuses so much on the rights of victims, why has no one truly addressed the plight of many divorced men in the United States?

In researching this book, I discovered that a quiet revolution is indeed starting to take place. Increasingly, fathers' rights groups are springing up around the country in an effort to help men help each other. For the first time, divorced men have someone to talk to other than their bartender. But these groups customarily deal with only the emotional and psychological aspects of divorce.

The purpose of this book is different. Although it will point out the emotional trauma unique to husbands in divorce, this book will focus more on explaining how the legal system really works; how men can protect their economic assets; how to obtain custody of the children if you so desire; how to obtain liberal rights of visitation; and how to determine whether your attorney is competent.

My intention is not to attack women, who must face their own problems during a divorce, often against great odds. And, obviously, I represent many women in my practice. However, my main focus here is to assist husbands and fathers with those divorce issues unique to their gender. This is intended to be a sourcebook for dealing with divorce. It assumes that every divorce is contested, even when the lawyers style it as "uncontested." In short, the book views the process of divorce as a competitive struggle in which there are two participants and where eventual victory goes to the party who has better prepared for the struggle and who has a better understanding of the overall system. To "win" at divorce, a husband must take *control* of the proceedings in an effort to get what he is entitled to.

Ultimately, this is a book of strategy. In its dollars and cents approach, every word is dedicated to assisting you in emerging from your divorce with your sanity and economic assets relatively intact. Women as well as men can benefit from the book's approach. Some of the suggestions contained herein may impress readers as harsh, possibly distasteful. But war isn't the only thing that's hell.

Divorce is typically a nasty business. Emotions usually run too high for it to be otherwise. My hope is that this book will assist the Jacks of this world in obtaining a level playing field. Only the Goddess of Justice is required to wear a blindfold. Not the participants.

CHAPTER 1

What to Do Before
You See a Lawyer

Let us assume that you have decided to initiate a divorce
from your wife. Perhaps you have come to realize that you
both are genuinely incompatible and that your constant
bickering has made the home a hateful place for you and
your children. Or possibly you suspect your wife of having
an affair. Maybe she has brought up the issue of divorce
on more than one occasion.

Don't think you can simply call a lawyer, park the problem in his lap, and sit back to wait upon events. If you
want to obtain a divorce that is fair to you and your children, you personally have a lot of work to do.

First and foremost, you must understand that once the
dreaded word "divorce" rears its ugly head, your relationship with your wife automatically becomes an adversarial
one, even if it was not before. Most marriages are economic partnerships and therefore involve common assets
such as joint bank accounts, joint investments, and real estate owned as husband and wife. Even if you secretly hope

for reconciliation with your spouse, your first step must be to safeguard those assets. Divorce does strange things to the nicest of people. The most even-tempered wife can become surprisingly vindictive, particularly if she is being coached by savvy friends or an aggressive attorney.

When a man first faces the issue of his divorce, he may be hamstrung by his conditioning. Men are taught by society to be polite toward women. They learn that although it is permissible, even encouraged, for them to be aggressive in most aspects of their lives, it is wrong to be combative toward women. Men are conditioned since childhood to suppress their feelings and emotions.

Statistics show that it is the wife who starts legal action in more than 90 percent of all divorces. Thus, the husband finds himself behind the proverbial eight ball right from the start. If he is not careful, he will find himself reacting to his wife's demands rather than pushing his own forward.

In today's world, you as a man simply cannot afford to abdicate your traditional role as the aggressor. The economic consequences of divorce are enormous and will demand your keenest competitive instincts. There are a number of steps that you can take in the beginning that will assure you a level playing field later on.

Timing Is Everything

Your child support and maintenance (alimony) payments will be based upon your present income. Consequently, it is in your best interests to try to delay pursuing a divorce until such time as your income and assets are at a low ebb. Perhaps you are self-employed and the sluggish economy hurt your business this year, but prospects look promising for the next couple of years. If this is the case, it is in your economic interest to initiate the divorce action immediately.

Maybe this approach makes you feel that you're being unduly harsh and that you're depriving your children of proper support. The first thing you must understand is that the divorce system is unfair to men. The system is not there to help you and, contrary to feminist rhetoric, there are few protections afforded you. Therefore, you will have to help yourself.

You must understand that if you fight the system, you are not fighting your children. Your wife and others may attempt to work on your emotions. They will argue that your tough tactics are indeed hurting the children. This is nonsense: Your children do not leave you voluntarily; the system takes them away. Your children do not destroy your standard of living. But the system will destroy you economically if you let it.

You do not penalize your children by seeking a $500 child support order from an unfair system. Remember: You can always pay more but the system won't allow you to pay less.

If you have a $500 child support order, you may be capable of paying $1,000. If you have a $1,200 child support order, however, you're in big trouble if you can't afford to make the payments.

The basic theme of this book is that *you* should seek to control only the divorce process, not your wife or the system, both of whom must be regarded as your adversaries in this limited context.

Let us assume that you have made a private decision in favor of divorce, and your wife, while suspicious that you're up to something, has not yet made any moves toward starting her own action. You must carefully consider the following strategies, tailoring your ultimate decisions based upon your own assessment of your wife's personality.

Bank Accounts, Credit Cards, and Other Assets

Go to the bank immediately and close both your joint checking and savings accounts. If you do not, you run the risk of your spouse cleaning out the accounts. The purpose of this tactic is not to spite your wife. You are only trying to protect yourself.

You cannot secrete this money—that would be a form of theft—but you can safeguard it. Simply put the money in another account under your name alone and then maintain a detailed record of how that money is spent. This way you have protected your money but can later prove to your wife's attorney that the funds were not squandered. Later, when tempers have cooled and the parties have reached some temporary truce, you can write her attorney a check reflecting her share of the bank account, particularly for those moneys she earned herself.

In Chapter 4 I discuss other ways of fairly accounting for your wife's money. The lesson to retain, however, is that *you* must win the inevitable race to clear out the joint accounts.

Notify *in writing* all credit card companies and department stores that you are canceling their credit cards, and that you will not be responsible for your wife's charges after a certain date—choose a date sooner rather than later. There is no legal requirement that you give them a reason. Mail the notification by certified mail and, as always, keep copies of everything you mail to anyone.

This action removes a powerful temptation from an angry wife. I once handled a case where my client had informed his wife that he wanted a divorce. In a vindictive fury she hit the department stores that same day and proceeded to run up charges of more than $20,000. In the end, I was able to argue convincingly to the court that her share of the final property settlement should be reduced, but that did my client little good in the short term.

If your spouse has joint access to safe-deposit boxes, re-move the contents before she does. Typically, people keep cash, stocks, bonds, and jewelry—all very liquid assets—in a safe-deposit box. Again, the key is not to hide these assets but only to protect them. The strategy is de-fensive in nature. Later, you can both agree as to who placed what in the box. At the very least, you should in-ventory the contents you have removed in the presence of a neutral third party.

I have heard of many other stratagems concerning safe-deposit boxes, especially when the two parties have set out to hurt each other. For example, the husband visits their box and removes all the contents. Then, in a display of evident gentlemanly behavior, he notifies his wife as to what he has done. She then rushes to the bank to check the box. Later in court when the wife's attorney claims conversion of assets, the husband's attorney can "inno-cently" show that the bank records indicate that the wife was the last person to have visited the box. Obviously, she must have removed the contents!

I do not recommend this tactic, because it assumes that the wife's attorney will neglect to ask the husband under oath whether he in fact cleaned out the contents. It fur-ther assumes that the husband will be comfortable with perjuring himself.

You may have a valuable coin or stamp collection. Re-move it immediately and consider selling it to a friend for a nominal sum with the understanding that you can repur-chase it after the divorce. Make sure you have a notarized bill of sale available. Without having the opportunity for an appraisal, it will be very difficult for your wife's attor-ney to prove what the collection is really worth.

This tactic can work against you, too. If you don't re-move your cherished collection, you will have to live with the other side's appraisal of what it was worth.

Or worse. I know of a woman who boasted about having pulled the proverbial wool over her ex-husband's eyes. It

seems her husband's father was a renowned painter and
many of his valuable works graced the walls of his son's
home. The artist's "mistakes" and lesser canvases collected dust in the garage. Knowing that her husband
couldn't tell the difference between a Rembrandt and a
billboard advertisement, this woman gradually replaced
the valuable paintings with less valuable works from the
garage. She said the process took more than six months
and her husband never caught on. Later, well after their
divorce, she sold her treasures through intermediaries for
a whopping price.

People often fight bitterly over possessions, no doubt in
misplaced anger at the other spouse. The extraordinary
fight over house and contents in the movie *The War of the
Roses* didn't faze divorce lawyers. I once represented a
woman who hated her husband for announcing he wanted
to start a new life without her. She fought him every inch
of the legal process (paying me handsomely for my efforts)
until she and her husband reached the very zenith of ab-
surdity. Each refused to part with two antique candlesticks the couple had purchased together in Russia.
Motions were filed, oral arguments heard, briefs re-
searched, all on the sole topic of who should receive the
candlesticks. Finally, I suggested to my client that *I* simply buy her another set of candlesticks—it would be far
cheaper for her. She refused. I was haughtily informed
that it was the principle of the thing. At long last, after
great expenditure of money and time, a judge resolved
the dispute in Solomon-like fashion: each side received one
candlestick.

Commentators tend to blame divorce lawyers for the
frustrations inherent in contested divorces, but I believe
that unreasonable clients can exacerbate the process far
more than the occasional unethical lawyer.

If your spouse is named as a beneficiary or executrix in
your will, it's essential to have a new will drawn up immediately.

Inventory Your Assets

Inevitably, in divorce, contentious conversations arise between spouses as to what was in the house before one spouse sold everything off. If you cannot prove that the dining room was once replete with Ethan Allen furniture, you're going to be out of luck in court.

Therefore, I counsel husbands who must leave the marital residence to go through the house thoroughly and make a list of all items that are easily sold and their values. Consider videotaping each room in the house from a number of different angles. If your wife questions this sudden interest in cameras, tell her you are making a record for insurance purposes.

If you are forced to leave the house without taking any property, it is not advisable to break the new locks your wife has installed in order to retrieve your property. Have your lawyer negotiate the return of the items or instruct him to file a motion in court. If your wife has a new residence, it is against the law for you to break in to retrieve your own property.

If you think your wife has hidden some of your assets, there are a couple steps you can take. First, make sure your eventual settlement agreement contains a clause covering ownership of after-discovered property. Second, ask your lawyer to obtain a temporary restraining order prohibiting any transfers of marital property. You will have to move quickly before the trail grows cold.

Change the Locks

Where one spouse deserts the other, I am often asked by the remaining spouse whether it is permissible to change the locks. The short answer is yes with the proviso that you'd better not later allege desertion. Your wife can convincingly contend that she didn't abandon you—you denied her the opportunity to return home.

Lower Your Standard of Living

If you are a man who fears divorce clouds are on the horizon, you would be prudent to take stock of your standard of living, and determine whether you have been unduly generous with your wife and family.

For example, is your wife a clotheshorse? Does she own dozens of suits and dresses, many hats and shoes? If so, rest assured that she will argue in court that this style represents her standard of living. Worse, she will contend that you must now continue to maintain her in the style to which she has grown accustomed.

If you have sufficient time before divorce proceedings are initiated, try to do everything in your power to reduce your wife's personal spending lest you be forced to continue paying the bills after your divorce. Talk down your income, moan about your expenses, but do everything possible to lower your standard of living. A lot of men in a bad marriage buy their spouses expensive gifts and luxuries just to "buy" some peace or to assuage their guilt. This approach is not only shortsighted, but may haunt these men for the rest of their lives.

Always keep in mind that your wife is about to become your legal adversary. While you must not do anything wrong or illegal, you are within your rights to safeguard your assets. In addition to following the steps noted earlier, you should collect all your family's financial documents—tax returns, bank statements, deeds, wills, and such—so that your lawyer will have the necessary information.

More important, your wife and her attorney must now face the preliminary obstacle of estimating your financial worth and the true extent of your marital property, without ready access to your papers. If your wife was the type of individual who was uninterested in the family financial status, don't start educating her now by leaving a paper trail!

The steps you take at the outset of a divorce often dictate the outcome of your case.

Talk to Your Financial Adviser

At my first meeting with a client I advise him to immediately contact his financial adviser, broker, or accountant, especially if the client owns securities, dividend investments, real estate, and other assets. A good financial adviser can suggest many ways to rearrange your investments or transform them into ready cash, thus salvaging assets from the rapacious grasp of your wife's attorney.

Such an adviser may well send you back to your attorney with the recommendation that you place a portion of your assets in a trust for the children, effectively withholding them from your wife and lowering your disposable income. There are any number of financial "dodges" available that can fit into your overall legal strategy. The key is assembling the proper team to represent you. So, when you take those initial steps to hire a good lawyer, remember that you need to retain an experienced financial adviser as well.

If you are the principal owner of a closely held corporation, there are many ways to manipulate your finances to disguise the true extent of your assets. Talk to your accountant; you may be able to charge personal expenses to the corporation. Or the corporation can retain earnings that will keep your income distribution at a low level. Or expense account disbursements can be fudged. Perhaps you can take out a loan from your retirement fund and "forget" to repay it.

Some of these dodges may be deemed illegal, so make sure your accountant is knowledgeable. As with your choice of lawyer, however, ascertain that he or she remains aggressive and protective of your interests.

Did you take out any loans for personal or business use in the past? If so, you probably filled out sworn financial statements where, in an effort to impress the bank, you inflated the extent of your assets and overvalued your true financial worth. In the hands of your wife's attorney, these statements could seriously harm your case. Make sure that your lawyer knows about these "time bombs" so that he can take steps to keep the hunters off the scent.

If you have a salary increase coming, an overdue bonus or a commission check, see if your company can defer payment. Try to win your employer's sympathy for your plight. Some bosses will go to surprising lengths to help out a valued employee. By suppressing current income, you will be making yourself a smaller target.

In this chapter I have outlined some of the preliminary steps you can take to protect yourself and your possessions. Always keep in mind, however, that divorce is a legal process. At some point—preferably early—you are going to need the counsel of a professional to guide you through the minefield that lies ahead.

Chapter Checklist

1. Recognize a contested divorce for what it is—a fight.
2. Lower your standard of living.
3. Consider closing joint bank accounts.
4. Cancel the credit cards.
5. Empty safe-deposit boxes.

6. Remove or sell cherished possessions.
7. Change your will.
8. Make a list of your assets.
9. Consider changing the locks.
10. Contact your financial adviser.
11. Postpone salary increases.

CHAPTER 2

Choosing a Lawyer

Choosing a lawyer is not unlike choosing a mate. And since you have proven you are not exactly adept at making such choices, I suggest you attend closely to the following.

First of all, if you want to win your divorce you must find a lawyer who is trustworthy and reliable, as well as experienced. There is no foolproof prescription to finding such a lawyer, but they do exist. It's your job to find one.

Don't even consider representing yourself, unless you have no possessions, income, or interest in the outcome. Being your own lawyer is the surest path to disaster.

Do you need to hire a bomber? It depends. If you don't have children, substantial property, or complex issues, the general practitioner down the street will probably be more than capable of handling your divorce. However, if your instincts tell you that you need quality advice, then don't hesitate. Hire the best lawyer you can afford even if his or her initial retainer causes you to blanch, particularly if your wife has hired someone equally respected. The consideration your case will receive in court—and the respect of your wife's attorney—often is directly related to your attorney's reputation in the legal community. You do not want to hire an inexpensive lawyer and thereby obtain an expensive divorce.

How to Find an Attorney

Spend some time researching the right attorney. If your first notice of a divorce is a letter from your wife's lawyer, followed up by various threats "to settle or else," don't be intimidated into making a quick decision. As with most things in life, a quick decision is a wrong one.

There are many ways to go about finding a qualified attorney. One of the most common is to use personal referrals from friends who have been divorced. What kind of job did their attorney do for them? What about their spouse's lawyer? Who seemed to hold the upper hand in negotiations?

The *Martindale-Hubbell Law Directory,* available at the public library, lists attorneys by specialty in every geographic location. Also, most local bar associations have a lawyers' reference service. Tell them you're looking for a lawyer with expertise in divorce law and they will give you a few names, but they cannot recommend one attorney over another. (Bar associations no longer provide minimum fee schedules because they have been found to be violative of the antitrust laws.)

The disadvantage of the *Law Directory* or Bar Association route is that they make no independent check on the credentials of the attorneys listed with them. Typically, a lawyer professing a specialty in the matrimonial area simply pays a fee to these services, which then add the lawyer to their lists, no questions asked. With no one checking up on these attorneys, there is no way for the consumer to be sure the attorney is in fact knowledgeable about divorce.

Beware of lawyers who advertise in the tabloids that they will handle your case for $350 or some such figure. This low number is employed strictly as a lure to get you in the door. Later you will find that "unanticipated" personal contact and litigation costs will revise that estimate significantly upward.

Another method of finding a divorce lawyer is to contact a local men's rights group. Often they will recommend certain attorneys who profess expertise and support of men's rights in divorce. Again, you can never be completely sure if the claims of these attorneys have been scrutinized.

My personal recommendation, and the method I follow when seeking a lawyer in another specialty, is to ask other lawyers for suggestions. Chances are you have a friend or a relative who is a lawyer. Perhaps your cousin is a tax lawyer with a big firm in the city. Ask him or her to do some of the legwork for you, by making some calls to colleagues. In discussing the qualifications of another attorney, a lawyer usually will be more forthcoming to another member of the bar than to a layperson. If you find that the attorney you are considering enjoys an excellent reputation among his or her peers, you can reasonably assume that you're making a good choice.

Interviewing the Attorney

Once you obtain recommendations, make appointments with two or three attorneys. Some lawyers charge their hourly rate for a consultation, whereas others accept a reduced rate. Many charge nothing at all for an initial interview. But don't go only to the attorney who waives the initial fee. By looking for a bargain you may miss meeting the professional best suited for your case. Always make sure to ask about that initial fee. As will be emphasized throughout these pages, it is your money. Don't ever forget that.

Your interviews with prospective attorneys are protected by lawyer-client privilege, and all your discussions, however preliminary, are confidential. A man I knew was sufficiently calculating to use this privilege as a weapon. He discovered that there were only three leading divorce lawyers in his town and realized that his wife was likely to retain one of them. Before she got started he immediately scheduled interviews with all three himself, finally selecting one as his advocate. The remaining two were barred from representing his wife because the husband had divulged information to them. The wife was thus relegated to hiring a second-tier attorney who was not her first choice.

Imagine that you are seated in an attorney's office for your first consultation. You are in a confused, emotional state. In addition, you probably have had little dealing with lawyers prior to the divorce. Maybe you even feel somewhat intimidated.

It is vital that your first interview be a two-way exchange of information and philosophies. You want to get to know your lawyer, and he should be interested in finding out about you. The lawyer will ask you to describe your marriage in a nutshell—its length, the number and ages of your children, the family finances, the jobs of both spouses, and your respective backgrounds.

Then the lawyer will want to know what led to the decision of one or both parties to seek a divorce. It is important that you answer these questions as frankly as possible. Your lawyer can help you only if you relate *all* the facts, favorable and unfavorable. Try to "improve" your story and you will only end up hurting yourself. You will also find that the mere exercise of reciting the history of your marriage to a stranger will serve to clarify your own thinking.

Your lawyer will ask a lot of questions. Does your wife have an attorney? Has anyone moved out of the house? Are you supporting her? Was the marriage ever good? If so, what went wrong? How did each of you contribute to its breakup?

Your lawyer should spend considerable time asking questions about your wife's character and personality. Like a good general he will know that a psychological profile of your wife is almost as important as the facts of the case. Is she vindictive? Is she penurious? Maybe she will succumb to the threat of a protracted and expensive fight. What will her "bottom line" be in terms of what she expects out of the lawsuit? Perhaps her love of the house and her desire to retain it will compel her to be more reasonable in the division of the marital assets.

Similarly, make sure that your lawyer understands how far you are willing to compromise. If you are prepared to be generous on child support but unwilling to pay a dime in maintenance (alimony), tell your lawyer exactly that. If you feel you might be willing to take your name off the deed to the house provided your wife agrees not to pursue your pension, say so. If you need the new car for your business, let your lawyer know up front. Don't keep anything back. Allow your lawyer to be the judge of what is important legally.

Discuss the children. Talk about their personalities and how the divorce will likely impact them. What will their desires be concerning custody? Is it possible that they will require therapy? Can you afford that expense?

After you have explored the personal side of your marriage, be prepared for your lawyer to ask questions concerning your financial situation. While you won't be expected to bring records to a first consultation, ascertain that you have hard estimates for the lawyer's inevitable questions. You will be asked such questions as: What is your income? Bonuses? Pension or profit-sharing plans? Any stock options? If your wife works, how much does she

earn? What and where are the family assets? Their value?
What assets did you both inherit, before and during your
marriage? Do you anticipate receiving any financial wind-
falls in the near future?

The key, of course, is to be completely truthful. If you
try to hide assets or keep your wife in the dark by keeping your attorney similarly unaware, you will only damage
your case. Worse, if you lie to your attorney, you always
run the risk of the truth coming out later from opposing
counsel. Not only will you lose your attorney's trust, you
will probably lose your case.

After the attorney has asked his questions, it is your
turn to interview him. Don't hector or seek to impress
with your general legal knowledge. Even if you have read
up on the subject of divorce law (which is a good idea), you
know a lot less than you think you do.

Of course, you want to discover how much your lawyer
knows about matrimonial law. Don't simply ask, "How
much do you know about this area of the law?" The answer
will be predictable and useless. Instead ask what percentage of the attorney's practice involves matrimonial matters.
(Anything less than 50 percent should make you remember
a sudden appointment.) Ask how many cases the lawyer
has tried in the past year or so. If he has tried two or three
cases, that is a satisfactory number. If he replies, "I don't
try cases because litigation is a waste of time and money;
I negotiate wonderful settlements," he's trying to cover up
the fact that he doesn't know where the courthouse is. And
if he has no reputation for trying tough cases, rest assured
that your wife's attorney will see this as a weakness. If an
attorney is reluctant to try a case—and many of them are—
he will negotiate your case away in the settlement process.

You don't want a lawyer who is merely book-smart.
Your lawyer must be able to provide you with a practical
perspective on the particular issues presented by your
case. Child support ranges and property division guidelines can differ from county to county. See if the attorney

knows what those ranges are in the court in which your case will be heard.

If your case involves property transfers and other complex issues, make sure that your attorney or his firm is knowledgeable in the area of tax law. As will be explored in greater depth later, tax considerations can dictate much of your strategy.

Like every other profession or trade, attorneys come in all sizes and shapes. Some fall into predictable "types" which you should be wary of.

The Busy Man If your lawyer allows your interview to be interrupted by telephone calls and distracted secretaries, and seems to live in a sea of paper and files strewn about his office, steer clear. This type will never return your calls; will tell you nothing about the progress of your case until the eve of trial, and will make you think murderous thoughts.

The Equivocator This kind of attorney will respond to your inquiries with vague replies and reminders that nothing is certain in this universe. He always sees both sides to every question and seems convinced that your position is weaker than your wife's. He will answer the simplest questions with shrugs and will never offer any predictions or assessments of your chances of success on the various issues in your case.

The Terminator This contentious lawyer is the opposite end of the scale from the Equivocator. He will try to impress you with his macho ways. He is proud of never negotiating and knows only how to file pleadings. Beware of the Terminator. His love of combat could end up costing you plenty.

Perry Mason Most of us grew up watching Raymond Burr in the role of Perry Mason. Unfortunately, so did many lawyers. This type of practitioner is a star—or at least he thinks he is. This egomaniac views his clients as annoying but unavoidable stage props. He will handle your case, and maybe even win it, but you will have little involvement and your opinion will never be solicited. Stars can be like that.

My descriptions of these characters are only partially tongue in cheek. It is remarkable how many lawyers resemble these caricatures. If you feel the attorney you're interviewing falls into one of these categories, avoid that attorney like the plague. There are many lawyers out there who are true professionals and craftsmen.

You may find it helpful to make a list of your requirements in the selection of an attorney.

1. You want a lawyer who is honest and competent, someone who is interested in you and your family, not in the extent of your assets. Avoid predators.
2. You want someone willing to give you estimates of your chances of success on the various issues present in your case. At the outset these predictions will be necessarily hazy, but you're entitled to know your options. And you are entitled to having those options explained in laymen's language.
3. You need a lawyer who knows that men have feelings, too, and that women have no monopoly on that trait. Your lawyer needs to understand that you are feeling tremendous stress, but will probably be reluctant to talk about it.
4. Above all, you want a tough, uncompromising advocate who is willing to go the whole nine yards for you. You do not want a lawyer who is looking to negotiate a quick settlement, collect his fee, and proceed on his merry way. Your case is vitally important to you, and it requires a representative who is sensitive to this fact. Also, there will be times when you

may be tempted to succumb to the pressure your wife and her attorney will exert; your attorney must remain strong in order to support you during those stressful times.

5. You may be best represented by an attorney who prefers to represent men. Most attorneys will deny they have any gender preferences in clients, but don't believe them. Look for a lawyer who likes to go up against a system weighted in favor of women.

Some men have told me they prefer a female attorney on the theory that female counsel will win them points with a jury, and soften the impact when the attorney goes after the wife on cross-examination. Other men fear that a female lawyer will not be able to stand up to a tough male lawyer on the other side.

My experience indicates that this is a bogus issue. There are so many female lawyers today—both good and bad—that their novelty has worn off with judges and juries alike. The "toughness" argument doesn't hold water either. Some of the most aggressive attorneys I have encountered have been women. Bottom line: Look for a lawyer, male or female, who is honest and competent.

Every so often you can encounter a lawyer who is becoming *too* friendly with the other side, particularly his or her counterpart. Understandably, lawyers in a specialized discipline in a given geographic area sometimes get to know each other pretty well. It's okay for your lawyer to know, respect, and even like his adversary. It's quite another thing when he seems to have gone over to the enemy. One man described his situation this way: "As my case progressed, I gradually came to realize that my attorney was no longer vigorously representing me. There were far too many jokes and huddles from which I was excluded. In settlement negotiations, my wife's lawyer would browbeat me for being allegedly unreasonable, with only occasional protests from my lawyer. When it got to the point that my lawyer took me aside to say I was being too stubborn, I mentally fired him. From that point on, I simply made believe that he wasn't there and I hammered out the terms of the divorce agreement with my wife's lawyer one on one. I think I got a better deal than the one my lawyer was trying to negotiate. But I also think I would have done even better if I had competent counsel who was willing to support me."

Legal Costs

At the close of your consultation, bring up the question of costs. Don't be reluctant to discuss this subject. It's your money, and the lawyer should not be uncomfortable in responding to your questions as to how he proposes spending it.

If your case is a simple uncontested divorce with no true property or custody issues, an experienced lawyer should be able to quote you a lump-sum fee. That lump sum should cover the lawyer's time and the costs involved.

If your case is more complicated, your lawyer may be unable to quote an estimated fee. Don't interpret his vagueness as meaning he is trying to mislead you. An attorney is paid for his time. Often at the outset of a case he cannot predict how long it will take him to investigate your family's assets, how "difficult" the other attorney will be, and how much time will have to be spent in discovery and litigation. Consequently, attorneys tend to quote an hourly rate and request that a retainer fee be paid in advance. (If your lawyer proposes a contingency fee based upon what he is able to collect in maintenance, child support, and such, head for the door because this proposal is both illegal and unethical in most jurisdictions.) Typically, a lawyer will request a retainer to cover his first fifteen to twenty hours in the case and the initial filing fees.

If your wife was the breadwinner in the family, some

lawyers will ask you for a retainer only, and will agree to collect the balance of their fees from your wife.

Hourly rates vary widely throughout the United States. An attorney in New York City will charge more than his counterpart in Mobile, Alabama, but his expenses are proportionately higher too. The only way to find out if you are being overcharged is to ask recently divorced acquaintances what hourly rates they encountered. As suggested earlier, if you have already interviewed more than one attorney you will have a reasonable idea about the going rate in your locale. Find out if the attorney has a different hourly rate for office time and for court time.

In addition to the attorney's hourly rates you will have to pay disbursements. These costs are incidental in nature, but they can add up and they are not negotiable. You will typically be billed for filing fees, messenger services, telephone calls, photocopying, and postage. You will also be responsible for court costs such as subpoena fees, investigator bills, and court-reporter charges for depositions.

Other costs involve work performed on your behalf by other attorneys or paralegals. Usually their time will be billed at a lower rate than that of the attorney you retained. You will also be responsible for the fees of expert witnesses and private investigators if such services are necessary.

Obviously, lawsuits can be expensive. You must take on the role of watchdog over the costs of your case, because no one else will. The first thing you must do is analyze the retainer letter your lawyer will ask you to sign. (If he doesn't offer a letter agreement, make sure *you* send him one.) Ascertain that the letter lays out your exact financial arrangement for the handling of your case. If you're unclear about something, ask questions.

Today, Fortune 500 companies hire outside consultants to analyze and question the legal bills presented by their outside counsel. Billing departments make mistakes and lawyers can be negligent in the way they record their time.

Look for the hidden costs. Did you know that the minimum time most lawyers record is a quarter hour? Thus, if your lawyer calls simply to say, "Send me last year's tax return," that three-second message will show up as a quarter-hour billing increment on your bill. This practice is rarely questioned by clients, but this does not mean you have to accept it. Insist that billing must reflect actual time expended.

Now that you're aware of this "hidden cost" you will understand why you should keep your telephone calls with your attorney to a minimum. Those pleasant conversations about the weather and the NFL season are costing you money! Be polite, but keep your conversations focused on the specifics of your case. Similarly, don't spend a lot of phone time crying on your attorney's shoulder. It's cheaper to hire a therapist if you're looking for emotional support. And it's probably a good idea for you to keep a log of the time you spend on the phone with your attorney.

If an idea or question suddenly occurs to you, it may be more cost-effective to send your lawyer a note than to call him.

If the lawyer's secretary answers a question for you, make sure his or her time doesn't show up on the bill. If it does, you're getting gouged.

Ask for itemized monthly bills. Young associates at law firms are under tremendous pressure to bill their time. If you feel that an associate billed an inordinate amount of time for drafting a simple motion, ask why. Why should you pay for an inexperienced, bumbling associate?

Make sure your retainer is refundable. If your case is settled quickly, or you reconcile with your wife, you're entitled to a refund of a portion of that retainer you paid up front. Some retainer agreements don't provide such protection and a greedy lawyer will dare you to sue him.

Remember, an honest lawyer will not be offended by

reasonable inquiries concerning his bill. At the same time, take special care that you don't nag him or her over trifles. Some element of your relationship with your attorney must be based upon trust.

Working with Your Lawyer

Arrive for all sessions with your attorney armed with notes to make sure that you cover the points you want discussed. Don't waste your time and his in extraneous conversation. Get to your points expeditiously, and try to be as businesslike as possible. Have all your personal and financial papers organized before the attorney even asks.

When discussing the strategy of your case with your attorney, don't be afraid to admit that you don't understand something. The law can be confusing, so don't be intimidated by its complexities. In my experience, the brighter the individual, the less afraid he or she is of disclosing ignorance.

Ask your lawyer for photocopies of all substantive pleadings and correspondence in your case. Although this presents a minor additional expense, it protects you against your lawyer losing your file folder, which happens more often than you might imagine.

During the course of your case your lawyer will send you many documents, usually requiring your review and signature. Don't do a fast shuffle on these papers. *Read every word.* Numerous problems later crop up as a result of poorly worded agreements and divorce decrees. Lawyers make mistakes, and you must painstakingly check everything that your lawyer does. Otherwise you can end up paying for his mistake.

Set ground rules about communication during the case. Ask your lawyer how often he will be calling you. If you have a weekend emergency—and these occur quite often in bitter matrimonial disputes—can you call your lawyer at home?

Obviously you don't need to be kept apprised of all the legal maneuvering that takes place between opposing counsel. At the same time you will become apprehensive if you hear nothing from your attorney for long stretches of time. Try to strike a balance: perhaps the lawyer's secretary or paralegal will agree to keep you current on a periodic basis.

Changing Attorneys

You did all your homework and invested a lot of time in selecting an attorney. Now, well into the case, you find that the relationship that should exist between attorney and client is just not there. Can you change attorneys? Should you?

First, I suggest examining your motives in switching lawyers. If it's simply that you don't like your lawyer, remember that you're not looking for a friend. If the lawyer is rude or temperamental, is boorish behavior sufficient reason to switch attorneys in the middle of a case? The attorney-client relationship is not a social one. If you dislike your lawyer, but nevertheless feel that he can represent you aggressively and competently, think carefully before deciding to change.

However, you must change attorneys if you believe that he is guilty of any of the following:

1. He is colluding with your wife's attorney.
2. You're spending money and seeing no activity or results.
3. He doesn't communicate with you unless he's looking for money.
4. He ignores your instructions without offering adequate explanations.
5. He's too busy to devote himself to your case.

Be careful how you go about changing attorneys. Before another lawyer will agree to take on your case that lawyer will want to be assured you have severed your connection with the first attorney. Thus, you must first find a second attorney willing to invest the necessary time for your type of case. Only then should you inform your present attorney that you are going elsewhere.

If you fire your attorney, your retainer fee usually will not be refunded. You may wish to guard against this eventuality in the initial retainer agreement.

Be prepared to pay off the first attorney immediately. Most jurisdictions recognize that a lawyer has a lien on his case file, and he will not release it to a second attorney until he is paid in full.

Note that it is more difficult for your lawyer to leave you than vice versa. He will need your permission or the consent of a judge before he can withdraw from a case.

Keep in mind that, although you have retained a lawyer, his assistance only goes so far. He can advise how to win your case legally, but you alone must deal with the emotional issues: moving out of the house or staying put, your children's well-being, your spouse's retaliatory tactics, the family finances, and every other problem that can arise in this situation.

Chapter Checklist

1. Hire the best lawyer you can afford.
2. Devote time to finding a lawyer.
3. Interview a number of lawyers.
4. Evaluate their fee structure, competence, and ability to instruct and listen.

5. Get a good understanding as to all anticipated legal expenses.
6. Ask for itemized monthly bills.
7. Make sure your retainer is refundable.
8. Take notes when meeting with your lawyer.
9. Ask for copies of all substantive pleadings filed in your case by both sides.

CHAPTER 3

The Home Becomes a Battlefield

Harry was incensed. Even in the somber confines of my law office, the knowledge of his wife's adultery rendered him nearly inarticulate with rage. "I found out yesterday that she would bring him into our bedroom while I was away at work," he moaned. "What if our son had come home early from school? I can't stand the sight of her. I'm moving into a motel tonight."

I sympathized with Harry's outrage, but counseled him not to act precipitously. I understood how hard it was for him to remain near his wife, but I had to point out that her lawyer might later argue that Harry's departure constituted an abandonment of his wife and family. A clever attorney could fudge the crucial distinction that Harry had left the marital residence *in response* to his wife's infidelity. And Harry could find his chances of obtaining custody of his children or possession of the house severely compromised as a result. Subsequently, Harry did move out, but only after we had obtained the written consent of his wife.

I try to impress upon my clients that their early actions can have unforseen legal repercussions for many years to come. In another example, after the legal fireworks started but without informing his attorney, Bob drove his wife and children to the airport. He thought it best that the children stay with his wife's parents while the lawsuit heated up. Bob's interpretation of this decision? He had nothing against his in-laws—his grievance was with their daughter. In fact, he felt rather noble in placing his children's emotional well-being above his own selfish interests.

His wife's lawyer had an entirely different interpretation. She later argued in court that Bob and his wife had evidently reached an informal agreement giving custody of the children to the wife. Otherwise, why had he been so quick to give them up? Was it not odd, argued the lawyer, that a husband who now asks for custody was so quick to relinquish it—and to his wife's parents—at the very beginning of the dispute?

The point is that entirely selfless acts can take on a different complexion in the hands of an experienced lawyer. That's the lawyer's job. The husband's job is not to give her material.

Divorce Goals

The husband must keep his eye on the ball at all times. He must temporarily shelve his emotions and never lose sight of his divorce goals.

"Divorce goals" may sound incongruous, but every plan must work toward clearly defined objectives. For example, your goals may be to obtain custody of your children, possession of the vacation house, and control of the family business. If you feel the marriage is dead, don't waste time stabbing the corpse. Instead, concentrate on achieving your goals.

If you storm out of the house in a rage, you may feel better temporarily, but you have driven your wife right into the arms of the enemy—her lawyer. You have given her no choice. If you stomp out with threats of dire consequences, everyone she consults is going to stand up and cry out in unison: "Get a lawyer now!" Not good strategy from your perspective.

Therefore, hard as it might be, try to remain cool and collected. Be a gentleman. No matter what the provocation, turn a deaf ear to invitations to fight. If your wife wants to tussle in the gutter, resist the temptation. In the context of divorce, quarreling gets one nowhere.

Until you have a formal, written agreement, don't move out of the house, even if asked to leave (and you will be). By maintaining the status quo, you are dodging the abandonment ploy. Moreover, your continued presence may upset your wife's psychological equilibrium. She's already emotionally taut. With any luck, she can't stand the very sight of you. By hanging around, you may force her into making mistakes.

Keep your eyes and ears open. You're not in your own home any longer—you're a spy in the enemy camp. If you anticipate a long and dirty fight with your spouse, this is the time she and her lawyer will be formulating their offensive. This is also the time that she will surreptitiously call friends to enlist them as witnesses against you.

In this period you will be observed very closely indeed by neighbors and acquaintances. If you act as normal and friendly as possible, you may defuse your spouse's allegations that you are some kind of ogre and, more important, you may disarm potential witnesses against your cause.

Another reason for remaining in the house: you may get a feel for the relationship between your wife and her attorney. How diligent does her lawyer seem? How often does the lawyer call? Does your wife appear to have input in the conversations? Does she seem to accept everything the lawyer says? Any observations you draw may help your own lawyer in formulating your strategy.

Assuming your wife is going to try for sole custody, she is going to have to prove in court that you are an unfit father. Proof means hard evidence, not unsubstantiated allegations. She will need sworn testimony, photographs, and documents that support her position. Therefore, if you drink heavily or use drugs, eliminate or diminish these activities pronto. If you persist, don't be surprised if those empty liquor bottles are being removed from your garbage every night by an outside party for use as evidence.

If you have a girlfriend your wife knows nothing about, please don't hand the other side a weapon. No one says that you must become celibate for the duration of your divorce, but it's wise to exercise caution.

Be alert for surveillance. You probably will never discover a professional tail, but fortunately few private detectives summon up memories of Sam Spade. Rediscover your rearview mirror. Is one car following you for a suspiciously long time? If you're walking to your girlfriend's house, reverse your direction suddenly and see if anyone follows suit.

All this may sound paranoid but don't forget that private detectives derive most of their income from matrimonial cases.

Don't suddenly become penurious. If you pay all the household expenses, continue to hand over these moneys to your wife, even if it sticks in your craw. The alternative—dramatically cutting back on her household budget— simply gives her attorney grounds to seek temporary support in court. If the judge is in a generous mood the day the motion is heard, he or she may well grant a significant temporary cash award to your wife. And you will be stuck with that amount for the entire duration of your case until a final award is entered.

As will be emphasized throughout these pages, don't allow the judge or the opposing attorney to control your checkbook. *You* must stay in control.

I do suggest confining your payments to items that are strictly necessary—such as food, clothing, school fees, and taxes. Cut back on the luxuries. All voluntary payments set a precedent. Later the lawyers and the judge will look back at this period of time to determine what the parties' standard of living was. Make sure that you are the one setting that standard. Make sure that you are in control.

Settling Your Own Case

As you read the preceding paragraphs, an uneasy feeling may have taken hold in the pit of your stomach. If you were not so aware already, you are now starting to understand that a bunch of strangers are going to control your immediate destiny—and make you pay handsomely for the experience! If you have any brains, you are wondering if it is possible to work out your own settlement with your spouse. This is the correct way of thinking, with certain provisos.

In 1521 King Henry VIII, who had some rather well-known marriage problems, asked, "Who does not tremble when he considers how to deal with a wife?" I suspect that Henry was alluding to the fact that women tend to be more articulate than men, particularly about emotional issues. If you want proof, turn on your television in the late afternoon. For whatever reason, women seem better equipped to debate issues with high emotional content.

Men act in the opposite way. Try surprising a male friend with an intimate confidence. He'll probably be so embarrassed by the encounter that you won't hear from him for months. Because most men are not accustomed to discussing their emotions, arguing emotional issues with your wife is not advisable.

Thus, if your wife attempts to berate you about your

current living arrangements, suggest that she have her attorney call your attorney. Sometimes lawyers can act as conduits in defusing emotionally volatile topics. Eventually the screaming should subside. When it does, test the waters. See if she is willing to discuss some of the issues in a relatively calm manner. If your wife proves malleable or susceptible to reason, I *always* recommend that my clients attempt to settle their own case before the lawyers get too involved.

The approach should go something like this: "Look, it's obvious that we don't get along anymore, but how about putting the reasons why aside for the moment. Let's see if we can resolve some of our differences ourselves as opposed to paying strangers a lot of money to do the same thing."

If she is receptive to this kind of pitch, run, don't walk, to your lawyer and find out the kind of parameters you are dealing with. That is, learn what a court is likely to decree and then attempt to get your wife to agree to something less. If, with the unseen guidance of your lawyer or a book like this one, you are able to agree on the specific terms of the divorce before your wife consults a lawyer, you have won the war.

To make the point another way, at the outset of a divorce dispute, if you can get past your natural anger, it's advisable to try to "finesse" your spouse into working out an informal settlement *before* she sees a lawyer. Unless your settlement terms are egregiously unfair, most lawyers will accept the conditions of a proposed settlement if both parties appear to agree. The average lawyer will not inquire too closely into the terms of a proposed agreement provided it doesn't appear to be too one-sided. You want her lawyer to see the potential for a quick fee with little effort on his or her part.

Divorce Mediation

Some couples prefer to avoid legal expenses by opting for divorce mediation. Divorce mediation clinics are increasingly touted as the best vehicle to assist couples involved in bitter marital property disputes. The avowed purpose of these clinics is to save the unhappy couple from the prolonged bloodletting of divorce litigation and high legal bills. Sounds good, but that's not the whole story.

First, keep in mind that the mediator represents *the couple* rather than each party. Therefore, he or she has no *obligation* to either party. Every mediator is intent upon putting together a quick settlement. If you hesitate for perfectly good reasons, you may be labeled as lacking sincerity.

Because mediation operates on the assumption that both parties are dealing in good faith, testimony is not given under oath, and there is no penalty for lying. Also, since mediation agreements are not legally enforceable, many times the mediator's work must be "undone" by the lawyers at a later stage.

Mediators typically obtain their degrees in the social sciences—psychology, therapy, or social work—and they often know little of the legal world they are venturing into. Although most mediators appear sincere, I believe they lack the requisite knowledge of divorce law, pension law, accounting practices, business and professional license valuation, real estate law, tax law, or any of the legal and business principles that necessarily underlie equitable distribution and communal property. In my opinion, divorce mediation should be considered only by those who have no assets and no issues in dispute.

If you live in a state where mediation is required before coming to court or if you have agreed to enter mediation voluntarily, treat the process seriously. In some states mediators have a great deal of power and can make recommendations to the court (which busy courts tend to simply adopt at face value).

A Final Warning

Until the divorce is finalized, remain wary. One of my clients was a womanizer for much of his marriage. John's philandering got so bad that one day his wife announced she wanted a divorce. She secured an apartment for which John paid the rent pursuant to a temporary court order obtained by the wife. John wasn't too upset because he remained in the marital residence with all the expensive furnishings. As the case proceeded, negotiations became very ugly with both parties and their attorneys fighting bitterly over every item of marital property.

One night John was surprised to run into his wife in a neighborhood restaurant. After a few drinks she appeared to thaw quite a bit with the result that the two ended up in bed back at the house.

Passion bred understanding. Before the night was over, they had even worked out the basics for a settlement agreement.

The next morning John left his wife still sleeping as he departed for work. Remember, John was very proud of his abilities with the opposite sex. Although he had no intention of getting back together with his wife (he had a newer model in mind), he was secretly pleased that, angry as she had been, she still could not resist his incredible sex appeal. When he returned home that evening he wondered if a candlelight dinner awaited his arrival.

You guessed it. John unlocked his front door to find that the entire house had been stripped completely bare. All the furnishings and possessions were missing and so was his wife.

In a contested divorce, inevitably the focus of the struggle will shift from the home to the courtroom. In a sense, this is why courts were invented—to provide an impartial forum where parties could sort out their differences. Once the lawsuit is initiated, however, it is imperative that your first steps be taken with assurance and calculation. Mistakes made at the outset of an action will haunt you long after the divorce is granted.

Chapter Checklist

1. Don't move out of the house without talking to your lawyer first.
2. The less emotional you are, the better your chances for a favorable outcome.
3. Define your "divorce goals."
4. To figure out your wife's strategy, keep your eyes and ears open.
5. Act normally toward friends and neighbors.
6. Correct your bad habits.
7. Continue to support your household but confine household payments to necessary items only.
8. Consider using your lawyer as a conduit to your wife.
9. Always try to settle your case short of litigation.
10. Approach the mediation process with caution.

4

The Opening Salvo

I am often consulted by husbands who want a divorce but at the same time do not wish to hurt their wives unduly. Many times a husband broaches the topic of divorce with his wife, but she simply refuses to respond seriously, perhaps hoping that the issue will go away. In this situation, a client will ask me, "What can I do? Our marriage is in ruins but she refuses to acknowledge it. Although I want a divorce, I don't hate her. And I definitely do not want a process server knocking on her kitchen door. We've gone through too much to treat her that way."

I usually suggest sending a letter that advises:

"Your husband has retained me in connection with certain marital problems which have arisen. Inasmuch as your husband is desirous of resolving these problems amicably, please have your attorney contact me promptly to discuss resolution of this matter."

Thus, the wife is alerted that (1) her husband is serious about getting a divorce (he hired a lawyer!) and (2) she better think about getting her own lawyer.

Some men, eager to secure every advantage in the divorce dispute, question actually recommending that the wife get her own lawyer. Isn't that like David suggesting to Goliath that he bring along a face mask, they ask? Not really, for one basic reason. The wife who is not represented by legal counsel will have no difficulty in later attacking the divorce agreement, even if the agreement truly conformed to her wishes at the time it was signed.

Any judge will simply assume that a husband who had the benefit of legal advice, when his wife did not, is guilty of overreaching. The man will be seen to have taken unfair advantage of his spouse. Therefore, the signed agreement in effect will be worthless and the negotiating process will begin anew. So it's in your best interest if your wife is represented by counsel (but one less competent than your advocate).

If letters are ignored, you will have no choice but to have her served with a summons and complaint. This may seem harsh, but the alternative—waiting months for your spouse to deal with the emotional issue of divorce—is unpalatable.

The summons and complaint are the initial pleadings in an action. They set forth the allegations upon which the requested relief is based and require that the defendant respond within a specified period of time. If the defendant fails to respond in time, the plaintiff can take a default judgment for the relief requested.

However, the taking of a default judgment at times is meaningless, because most courts are reluctant to grant one-sided divorces to deny a party her day in court. You may safely assume that your wife's attorney will have little difficulty in vacating the judgment.

Some husbands and wives have abandoned their spouse or simply wish to avoid service. If the process server cannot serve his or her papers in the normal fashion, the court can still grant the divorce. It will require that you make present some evidence that you attempted to find the missing spouse, after which you will have to publish the complaint in a local newspaper. After a statutory period of time (usually thirty days), if the other party has not surfaced, you will be granted a default divorce, commonly known as a divorce by publication. In this type of divorce, however, the court can only sever the marital relationship. It cannot decree child support or maintenance without hearing from the missing defendant.

Motions for Temporary Relief

Assuming that the two parties have "joined issue," as the lawyers say, or that the summons and complaint have been met with an answer, what happens next is one of the most crucial phases of the lawsuit. Inevitably, the wife's attorney will make a motion for temporary relief, meaning the attorney will ask the court for some particular relief pending the final judgment for divorce.

In essence the wife is telling the court, "My husband is the breadwinner and he controls the family finances. Currently, he is refusing to give me and the children enough money to survive on. Accordingly, I ask that the court issue some 'temporary' orders giving me 'temporary' custody, child support, maintenance (alimony), and curtailing my husband's rights of unfettered visitation with the children. Oh, by the way, to ensure a level playing field, please order my husband to pay my legal expenses."

In my estimation, these motions for temporary relief represent a most serious threat to the American husband. First of all, the hearing on such a motion occurs at the very beginning of the lawsuit, sometimes on as little as three days' notice. If the wife is the plaintiff, as is typically the case, her attorney may have had weeks to prepare her case and supporting evidence. But once the motion is served, the husband must whip together a hasty defense with the result that he often absorbs an early drubbing.

The hearing at which attorneys for both parties present their evidence is very informal. All the commentators laud informality because it sounds less procedure-driven. However, I believe this very informality presents a grave danger to the husband. What often happens is that overworked judges do not have time to read the affidavits, and instead rely upon the two attorneys' oral presentation to learn about the case.

The wife's attorney has a demonstrably easier burden to sustain. She argues that the court needs to protect the helpless wife and children and that her motion only seeks to preserve the status quo. The wife's attorney will disclaim any intention to prejudge the case; no, she seeks only to obtain protection for her clients "for the time being." As a result, the wife's attorney is portrayed as the protector of innocents and invites the judge to "do the right thing."

Conversely, the husband's attorney is usually burdened with the uncomfortable role of repeating over and over, "Your Honor, my client does not have the money or ability to meet these outrageous demands." This is a weak argument that runs dangerously afoul of accusations that the husband is a deadbeat. The usual result, depending on the extemporaneous skills of the husband's lawyer, is that the husband is saddled with a whopping financial burden *before anyone has passed judgment on the merits of the case.*

In light of the foregoing, make sure to bring a copy of your paycheck stub to court, even if no one asked for it. In addition, bring along a list of your fixed living expenses. More times than not, I have seen judges base their orders upon the sole evidence of the paycheck stub.

Another misconception about temporary orders is that

they are indeed "temporary." In the real world, the court order for temporary relief tends to become permanent. If the temporary award is significant, the wife's attorney will certainly argue during the divorce trial that the issues underlying the award had already been examined by a learned judge and, therefore, there is no reason to overturn the previous ruling.

This is a powerful argument. Judges are reluctant to overturn the decisions of other judges unless the husband can demonstrate some compelling reason. There is nothing in contemporary American divorce law that requires the husband to meet such a burden, but every matrimonial lawyer will agree that such a burden exists.

Unintentionally, the system administers a double whammy to husbands. The judge who hears the application for temporary relief will often grant a high award to the wife on the premise that the weaker sex must be protected. The judge undoubtedly reasons that the whole issue of support will be examined more fully at trial. But in reality, the trial judge is loath to disturb the previous judge's ruling, and so the husband is hit both coming and going.

If you earn more than your wife, which is still the norm in this country, you have the most exposure in a motion for temporary support. Therefore, as noted earlier, you must develop strategies to prevent the law from working against you.

The first step is to acknowledge that you have a responsibility to support both your wife and children. You and your attorney should try very hard to negotiate a temporary arrangement with the other side regarding support and payment of previously incurred marital debts.

If you followed my earlier advice, you will have closed out the joint credit cards. A simple letter will suffice, particularly if you mention the dreaded word "divorce"—still the quickest way to freeze a credit card account. Some disreputable attorneys actually advise reporting the cards as stolen, but such dishonesty will only hurt your credibility. (Also, what is to stop a credit card company from taking you at your word and issuing a new card to your spouse?)

Consider closing out joint bank accounts, and opening up a new account, along the lines discussed in Chapter 1. Another option would be to take one half the funds for your use (while maintaining scrupulous records concerning all expenditures) and place the other half in a separate interest-bearing account. Or the other half can be placed in your attorney's trust account with the written understanding he can negotiate a further division of those funds with the other side or make those funds the subject of a temporary motion, inviting the court's instructions as to allocation.

What you are trying to accomplish with these maneuvers is to provide for your family and prevent your wife from later arguing that you cut them loose without resources to survive on. You will also have the comfort of knowing your wife cannot spend these moneys without accountability. You retain control.

Prior to filing suit, you should also consider paying certain mutual debts, particularly those that will affect your credit. The debts will have to be paid anyway and you will look good to the court when your papers on the support motion show that you made such payments voluntarily.

If you have sufficient resources but your wife has none, you should consider paying your wife's attorney her retainer. It's safe to assume that the amount you eventually agree to pay her attorney will be a lot less than the amount the attorney would have requested in her motion for counsel fees. This way you retain some control over what you will likely have to pay, and her attorney will feel some goodwill toward you since (1) she has money in her pocket and (2) you have exhibited a willingness to be "reasonable." (Actually, you have done nothing of the sort.)

Of course, all your promises should be reduced to writing and signed by both parties and their attorneys. In

working out these early agreements you are also estab-
lishing some numbers (not unfair to you) that will become
the norm between the parties. Thus, if you later breach
the agreement, it is unlikely a court will impose new support numbers that are higher than were agreed upon. After all, didn't your wife and attorney sign an agreement
which de facto indicated this amount of support was sufficient?

It's not advisable to go the agreement route, however,
unless you plan on living up to its terms. You should be attempting to create an atmosphere of reason and cooperation, which can only help both parties. By playing games,
you run the risk of destroying your credibility with the
other side. The result is a lack of cooperation later on
when you need it.

In actuality, though, many cases are not guided by reason and end up in litigation. Too frequently, I have seen a
husband strike his colors at the conclusion of the hearing
on the motion for temporary support. Who can blame him?
He has just been smacked with a huge award for alimony
and child support. His wife has been granted temporary
custody of the children, and his access to his own children
has suddenly been severely limited. To add insult to in-
jury, perhaps he has been ordered to pay for his wife's legal expenses in addition to his own.

Very often the new financial and emotional demands
placed upon the husband can sap his will to resist his
wife's demands. Already destroyed once by the system, he
is reluctant to get in the way a second time. The case is
over before it has even properly started.

This is a gloomy but not exaggerated picture. Motions
for temporary relief must be taken very seriously. Here
are a number of ways in which to better protect yourself:

1. If you are the defendant, anticipate that the other
   side will be filing the inevitable motion for temporary relief. Prepare and document a defense that will

systematically refute your wife's inflated demands for financial aid. Not only will you stand a better chance of winning on the merits, but you will also be serving notice on the opposing attorney that she is in for a fight.

2. You have an obligation, legal and moral, to support your family to the best of your financial ability. Niggardly support payments will come back to hurt you at the hearing. Also, your obligation to pay support commences on the day you are separated from your family, *not* on the date the order is signed by a judge. Therefore, most support orders require that the father pay a lump sum for the period of time leading up to the support order. You can avoid this stipulation by voluntarily providing fair support allowances. If you fear that you might be too generous, place the excess amount in a bank account until such time as a judge determines the support award. This is a wise strategy once you realize that any excess you might have been voluntarily paying will *not* be returned to you.

3. Encourage your wife to seek work. The better her job, the more likely her pleas for support will fall on deaf ears.

4. Always ask for custody of your children, unless you feel that it's not in their best interests. Local courts look favorably upon fathers who seek custody of their children.

5. Generally speaking, alimony or maintenance payments are tax-deductible; child support payments are not. Try to get your lawyer to style as much of your support obligations as possible as being maintenance payments. If properly worded in the order, you will get the deductions while your wife must declare the payments as income.

6. Make sure your lawyer is not thinking purely defensively at the temporary support hearing. As long as

the judge is stuffing the order with items unfavorable to you, try to include some favorable wording from your perspective. Perhaps you're afraid your wife will later move to the state her mother resides in. Have the order state that it is prohibited for the wife to leave the state with the children. It won't hurt to include a few paragraphs stating she cannot disparage you in front of the children and that you must be consulted on all short-term decisions involving education, travel, health care, and such.

Hearings on temporary support can be abrasive. A lawyer who hails from the school of intimidation will seek every opportunity to humiliate or anger you. The purpose is twofold: (1) she can take your measure, seeing if you are easily ruffled; and (2) rough handling might intimidate you into settling the main case on their terms. Don't get caught up in the other lawyer's rhetoric. Be guided by your attorney's advice.

If it happens that your wife earns more than you or you are temporarily unemployed, by all means seek as much maintenance and support as you deem necessary. The feminist revolution has theoretically gender-neutralized our divorce laws. Joan Lunden pays $18,000 a month in alimony. Jane Seymour parts with $10,000 every month until 1994. And Jane Fonda shelled out $10 million! Therefore, put your male ego to the side, and let the law work in your favor for a change. But don't be terribly surprised to discover that many judges will be unreceptive to your petition. Men are much more likely to be brusquely told to go out and get a job.

Settlement Conferences

After the initial flurry of pleadings, one or both sides may suggest a sit-down meeting "to see where we are."

These settlement meetings often provide the forum for airing grievances and hammering out an agreement. In fact, most matrimonial cases begin and end in the lawyer's office. Other parts of this book deal with the substantive issues to be discussed at such a meeting, but the actual format of such a meeting is a natural topic at this juncture.

Prior to the meeting, you and your attorney will meet to discuss the issues relevant to your case and how they rank in importance to you. For example, your first priority may be sole control of the family business, your second priority may be some form of joint custody and liberal visitation, third may be payment of minimal spousal support, the fourth to regain control of certain personal possessions and furniture. Assume that you are not particularly interested in staying in the family residence, you are willing to give her half your pension, and you will allow her the choice of the two family cars.

It is important that your attorney know whatever concessions you have in mind. If he knows how to bargain (something not taught in law schools), he will use these concessions as bargaining chips in order to obtain the desired outcome on the important issues.

At this early stage the discussions and concessions are not binding. If negotiations break down, you can go to court and argue from ground zero. After all, your reason for attending the meeting is to try to reach a quick and reasonable settlement and thereby save money on legal fees.

I prefer uncontested settlements if for no other reason than that the two parties should be making their own agreement rather than having it made by outsiders such as a judge or jury. If the other side makes unfair demands, however, you should feel no pressure to settle. If your spouse is not willing to be reasonable, you can resolve the matter in court.

Meetings of this type are informal. No record is maintained other than the parties' notes, and even that is optional. Typically one of the attorneys will have put together an agenda or list of issues and will suggest that the parties and counsel discuss these items individually. Sometimes immediate agreement can be reached on a particular issue, whereas an impasse may occur with another. If there is no quick agreement on certain items, the parties usually continue through the remainder of the list in the same fashion.

In this way, the parties have an opportunity to focus on the real issues separating them and, most important, the *reasons* behind their positions. In my experience, settlements always result when the parties truly listen to each other—with understanding comes reason. When parties are more intent on scoring points, the discussions unravel.

Always take detailed notes; never rely solely on your attorney's notes. This will help your attorney later in case he missed something and will give you a better understanding of exactly what has been agreed to around the table.

If you want to confer privately with your attorney, by all means speak up. If you're feeling emotional and need to take a break, that's also okay.

If the discussions are proceeding amicably, at some point some serious dickering will take place. This is the time when two parties who truly want a settlement "give up something to get something." I prefer to make the first serious offer. This way, I get to set the basic parameters for settlement and establish that certain items are nonnegotiable. In other words, this tactic allows me to select the playing field.

An astonishing number of attorneys fail to make the first offer, thus permitting me to protect my client on those issues he deems most important. I then look to receive a counteroffer. If, instead, counsel merely attacks my offer and suggests I make a new proposal, I always refuse because I am then bargaining against myself.

If the counteroffer is serious, after some discussion of its merits, I usually suggest that the parties confer privately with their respective counsel and then resume discussions. If the offers are not too far apart, one party should try to narrow the differences still further in hopes of resolving the dispute. If positions stiffen, the parties should adjourn the meeting for a week to allow opportunity to reflect.

Assuming an agreement is reached, your attorney cannot draw up a comprehensive settlement agreement on the spot. Since oral agreements generally are unenforceable, however, you don't want to leave the meeting without something to prove an agreement was indeed reached. Therefore, one of the lawyers should draw up a quick memorandum of settlement which briefly recites all the terms of the agreement, and both parties and their counsel should sign this memorandum.

Of course, if you are the one who is wavering and you want additional time to reflect, ask that the memorandum include a 48-hour "cooling-off" period, during which time you can renege.

Jurisdiction

Another initial consideration is where to sue for divorce. Every client of mine seems to have a friend who flew to Las Vegas, stayed in a hotel for a few weeks to establish residence, got a "quickie Nevada divorce," and returned home with a divorce decree valid in his home state. The inevitable question: why can't I do the same and avoid all this rigmarole my home state subjects me to?

The answer is that such a divorce has little weight. Nevada may be satisfied it has jurisdiction if you *resided* there for the amount of time specified in its statute, but before New York and most other states will accept the decree and give it full faith and credit under the Constitution, they must be shown that you were *domiciled* in Nevada.

There is a crucial difference between domicile and residence in the eyes of the law. A resident is someone who lives at a certain address, whereas a domiciliary is a person who considers that address his home. (A U.S. Foreign Service employee from Des Moines is stationed in Berlin. Berlin is his residence—Des Moines is his domicile.)

If you are not domiciled in Nevada, there is a very good chance that New York will not accept Nevada's jurisdiction and will set aside the decree.

We all hear about movie stars flying to Haiti or Mexico to obtain a divorce. Or both parties petitioning by mail through the agency of a lawyer in a foreign country. Again, your home state is under no legal compulsion to recognize the divorce. In my opinion, your spouse will have no difficulty in attacking the validity of such a divorce. (N.B.: In order for a divorce decree to be set aside, someone must contest it. If you are positive that your wife will forever remain satisfied with the terms and conditions of the foreign decree, you're safe.)

As your lawsuit proceeds, you will find that the law prizes logic. Lawyers and judges alike will recommend that you act "reasonably" and park your emotions outside the courthouse door. This is more easily said than done. Nevertheless, it is good advice. On the theory that forewarned is forearmed, the next chapter discusses some emotional problems typically encountered by litigants.

Chapter Checklist

1. If your wife doesn't want a lawyer, strongly recommend that she hire one.

2. Motions for temporary support and custody can destroy you. Treat them seriously.
3. Consider paying off certain mutual debts.
4. Consider paying for your wife's attorney.
5. Insist on written agreements.
6. Always ask for custody of your children.
7. Encourage your wife to work.
8. Don't be embarrassed to ask for alimony if you're entitled.
9. Always treat settlement offers seriously.
10. Beware of out-of-state or foreign divorces.

CHAPTER 5

The Emotional
Roller Coaster

Men have been conditioned to view emotions as so many impediments to a "normal" life, and traditionally have been uncomfortable in dealing with their emotions. Many men refuse to admit that feelings of depression or rejection are more than momentary phases. Consequently, a man who is suddenly confronted with the gut-wrenching trauma of divorce often is wholly unprepared. Since he possesses no tools to deal with the unfamiliar feelings overwhelming his life, he will hide behind the only defenses known to him: anger, alcohol, drugs, or work.

When individuals suddenly act irrationally, psychologists say that they are experiencing an "adjustment disorder." They find it difficult to make decisions, with the result that their judgments tend to be based on emotions rather than reason.

Let us assume your wife has left you for another man. Unbeknownst to you, she had had an ongoing affair with this man for months prior to your breakup. You vow to get even with both parties, particularly your wife.

In our brave new world of sexual freedom and womens' rights, this scenario is all too common. When a client, overwhelmed with the shame of being cuckolded, visits my office, I ask him one question: "Is your marriage over?" If the response is in the affirmative, I tell him then and there that it is imperative he get past his anger. He must move on with his life, placing his marriage firmly behind him.

Controlling Your Anger

There are many theories as to why anger is such a prominent feature of divorce. According to Dr. Scott Wetzler, Chief of Psychology at Albert Einstein College of Medicine:

> If there is one psychological truth about divorces, it is that they tend to be unnecessarily acrimonious. Anger poses the single greatest obstacle to making progress, legal as well as psychological. To think of love and hate as polar opposites is mistaken—they go together. We get angry at the ones we love, those who are nearest and dearest. In fact, anger is a sign of our continued love and involvement. From the psychological perspective, a relationship is severed only once it does not elicit strong feelings. Apathy and indifference are the psychological evidence of a dead relationship. Thus, persistent anger at a spouse is an attempt to perpetuate the relationship. Not only does anger blind the client from making a level-headed decision, it binds the client to their spouse (no matter how vehemently they claim they want to separate). It is frequently counterproductive for an attorney to encourage a client's anger at his or her spouse.

Dr. Wetzler also states:

> What makes divorce so difficult is undoing the intimacy which is established during marriage. A marriage changes an individual's identity and sense of self. There is a merging of two identities, a diminution of a sense of oneself as a separate human being, and the establishment of a communal identity which transcends the self. The boundary between "you" and "me" dissolves, and a "we" emerges. Thus, divorce entails the loss of that part of oneself which resides in the spouse.

You may remember the story of Barbara and Oliver Rose in the movie *The War of the Roses*. Their marriage began in multiorgasmic bliss only to end in the total destruction of their lives, home, and possessions. All because they succumbed to the feelings of anger and revenge lurking in every divorce. Danny DeVito, who plays Michael Douglas's lawyer in the movie, says at one point, "A civilized divorce is a contradiction in terms." But the lesson of the movie is *not* to allow feelings of anger to dominate the spirit of one's divorce.

Emotions can wreak havoc with your case. Although it's only natural that both parties are under a great deal of stress, it's vital to try to control your emotions at this time. Seek counseling from an experienced professional or member of the clergy, if necessary.

We live in a legal and moral climate where there is no interest in who was responsible for the breakup of the marriage. This is the no-fault age. When the Roman Catholic Church in the United States recently revised its definitions of what constitutes sin, the popular media's reactions varied from bemused detachment to outright scorn. The very principles of sin, guilt, and responsibility carry little weight in modern society. Your wife could be having sex on the Sears Tower and the judge could care less (unless you can demonstrate a deleterious effect on the children.)

Today, divorce cases are primarily property distribution cases. With the removal of fault considerations from our courts, the days of hiring private detectives to take pictures of surprised lovers in flagrante delicto are gone. Quite properly, most of our state legislatures decided to pull matrimonial law out of the sordid muck of lying and spying; presently divorce cases can be analogized to the dissolutions of business enterprises. You may wish to punish your spouse or blame her for the divorce, but the courts will be uninterested in determining the merits of these issues.

Matrimonial law does not contemplate moral vindication. The judicial system is not a parent surrogate, and the judge will not absolve you and your behavior during the marriage. To hope otherwise is to be unrealistic.

The style of divorce lawyers has changed, too. Today's matrimonial lawyer must be comfortable with analyzing a spread sheet, pulling apart a pension plan, finding assets, examining interlocking companies and directorships, and such. The old-timers tell me all the fun has gone out of divorce law, and they're probably right.

Of course, controlling one's anger is more easily said than done. Human beings are not automatons, and it is entirely natural for the aggrieved husband to want to "get even." The professional lawyer understands the reasons underlying his client's anger, but counsels him as to how that emotion can ultimately injure his case.

Courts will not tolerate unreasonable delays or a husband's refusal to honor his support obligations. Revenge is ultimately self-defeating, and outbursts in court directed against an unfaithful wife will only result in angering judges and perhaps prejudicing them against your case. Your wife's lawyer is well aware of this. Give her lawyer the slightest indication that your temper can be engaged, and she will be after you like a shark on the scent of blood.

Also, as will be explored in more detail later, you win or lose a divorce case based upon how well you negotiate. Any lawyer will tell you that a hot-tempered adversary inevitably self-destructs and makes mistakes. The same rule of thumb applies to the man who is annoyed at the entire system and, rightly or wrongly, perceives it as his enemy. To win at the negotiating table requires equanimity and level-headed behavior. This should never be forgotten.

Worry About Yourself

If you feel rejected, try to regain your self-confidence, either through group therapy (there are many excellent men's self-help groups) or by self-discipline. If your wife has left you, it simply means that she has decided her new life is most important to her.

Don't make the mistake of allowing her to determine the worth of *your* life. You are the sole master of your destiny. Try to stop blaming yourself, and get on with your life.

Treat friends' advice with circumspection. Accept their emotional support and home-cooked meals, but dodge the advice. Because no two divorces are the same, a friend's counsel, while well-intended, may prove misleading and inapplicable to your case. Divorce is not only a crisis for you: it was a watershed for the friend relating his story. There is a human tendency in telling a story to embellish, refine, and selectively remember. Your friend may draw conclusions at your peril.

Popular mythology paints the woman as the selfless partner in a marriage, eschewing a career for the burdens of family and motherhood while the father enjoys a dynamic life in the outside world. Most men I know would be shocked if they were told they were leading such interesting lives.

Men are tired of being told they are the problem. The psychobabble that passes for informed talk on television and radio shows unceasingly characterizes manhood as some kind of affliction to be overcome. Since none of us like being characterized as selfish hedonists, we overcompensate trying to be Mr. Right. You know him. He's the guy we all want to be. He can cook elaborate breakfasts, go coach Little League (where he is careful to instill in his charges at least three times an hour the dictum that winning is unimportant), jog back home, discuss meaningful intimate matters with his wife, cry a little, insist upon cooking dinner because the other coach passed on a new recipe, perform incredibly in bed, and the next morning conclude a unique acquisition deal at the office (which required no preparation the previous day).

The sooner men reject the impossible burdens society imposes, the sooner reality will return to the marriage relationship. This does not mean that women should relinquish their hard-won gains. But men should no longer be labeled the enemy. They should be allowed to stumble and fall and get up again, all without the attendant opprobrium of popular culture.

In the context of divorce, worrying about yourself means just that. Forget the boyfriend. Picking fights is for kids and is dangerous anyway. He did nothing that your wife didn't want to happen. And don't bore other women by comparing them with your wife. Let go of the past and take control of your life.

I have found that nothing infuriates a woman more than indifference. If your wife has left you for another, let her know in no uncertain terms that when she went out the front door it closed behind her forever. If she wants to bicker or try to justify her acts, don't buy into it. Maintain a pose of detached objectivity. Curl your lip in distaste. Your apparent indifference to her departure will infuriate her. Many women, raised on a diet of passionate soap operas, thrive on drama. Don't give her the satisfaction. Keep in mind Kipling's lines:

"If the wife should go wrong with a comrade, be loth
To shoot when you catch 'em—you'll swing, on my oath!
Make 'im take 'er and keep 'er: that's Hell for them both,
An' you're shut of the curse of a soldier."

Most divorces are the result of a breakdown in mutual affection between both parties, and both parties bear varying degrees of responsibility for the breakdown. Many individuals refuse to accept responsibility for their own acts, however. Because we live in an age that teaches it is always somebody else's fault—your parents, your teachers, your husband—don't be surprised if your wife blames you alone for the divorce: "It was all your fault." False stories and outright lies may be planted with your mutual acquaintances. Friends will start to give you strange looks because no one knows what went on behind closed doors.

If you become the victim of this kind of campaign, sadly there is little that you can do. Sometimes protesting too much tends to lend support to the stories.

You are probably best off remaining above the fray. It may be hard to prove, but most outsiders aren't that interested in other people's lives. One of the first things they tell you in Alcoholics Anonymous is that you're foolish to think all your acquaintances were obsessed with observing your every misadventure. Most people are kept busy worrying about their own problems. Therefore, don't get bogged down in worrying what others think. Move on.

Taking Responsibility

If you have left your wife for another woman, for reasons as basic as that she doesn't interest you anymore, you must acknowledge that you have caused her pain. You are going to feel guilt and this is natural. It is also understandable that your wife will be upset. If you have dropped a bombshell on her, she is going to run the gamut of emotions: anger, bitterness, fear of the unknown, depression. She will also fear that your new girlfriend is going to replace her as the mother of your children.

Although the emotional level will be high, it is your responsibility to own up to your actions, to admit to any hurt you may have caused, and to reassure your spouse that your intention is not to injure or humiliate her, and, certainly, not to interfere with her status as the mother of her children.

A word of caution: Before putting any acknowledgment of responsibility in written or formal form, it would be prudent for you to talk to your lawyer. An example: Recently, I heard a therapist expounding on this subject on a television show. Quite rightly, she pointed out that in the early stages of a breakup the emotions may be running so high that it is impossible for the parties to talk meaningfully to each other. The therapist recommended writing a letter to the other spouse, acknowledging one's own fault in causing the rupture and apologizing for any hurt visited upon the other. She particularly stressed the need to list the wrongs committed by the responsible spouse. The show host and other guests all but genuflected before this perceived wisdom. It was almost as if they were in church, and in a sense that is exactly where they were—in church bowing before the great god Psychobabble.

I am always amazed at the amount of nonsense that is projected across our airwaves on a daily basis. I for one was shocked by the therapist's advice. Her well-intentioned suggestion completely ignored the fact that divorce often takes place within the context of a lawsuit. I could only imagine being in court locked in a hotly contested custody battle when my adversary introduced into evidence my client's letter detailing in his own handwriting all his failures as a husband and father. I can assure you that my client would not harbor kind feelings toward that therapist!

Taking responsibility is one thing, but I should state here what should certainly be obvious by now. Never put anything in writing without talking first to your attorney. And if you're thinking of writing something pertaining to your marriage and you don't yet have an attorney, don't do it!

Guilt

If you were wrong, the key is to own up to your acts like a man but not to wallow in guilt. You simply cannot allow the emotional aspects of divorce to hinder your main goal—getting a divorce.

If your wife discovers your adultery and threatens to "take you for everything you've got," don't be intimidated. Here, the no-fault laws work in your favor. She will get her fair share of what is in the marital pot; that share will be determined by formulas and negotiation. Your adultery is not a factor.

Remember, however, adultery does introduce a psychological factor. For example, if you experience tremendous guilt when your philandering is unmasked and your wife is cunning enough to discern your guilty feelings, her lawyer can bank on the fact that you will be inclined to make considerable concessions in hopes of putting the problem behind you as soon as possible. Rely on your lawyer to protect you from yourself.

Many men, overly sensitive to what their neighbors are thinking, immediately decide to move out of the house. Again, some are feeling misplaced guilt. Guilt should never motivate decisions. It's a different story if you're moving to allow everybody, including yourself, some cooling-off space. If your attorney advises that it's okay, there's nothing wrong with seeking other living accommodations. However, I normally recommend against seeking a cheap apartment in a bad area of town, far away from the family, in a misguided attempt to save money.

In the first place, if you are located a great distance from your family, neighbors, and activities, you are going to be miserable. And why are you running away anyway? You don't need to act as though you have done something wrong. Stay local. By paying low rent in a run-down neighborhood, you risk having a court deem that amount of rent as representing the fair market rate for rentals in your area. Judges are not real estate brokers. When the judge is dividing up the marital property and determining who needs what, don't mislead the court as to how much rent you'll need for a decent apartment.

Therapy

Should you see a therapist? By all means. Raised on the myth of the tough American hero, many men find it difficult to contemplate discussing intimate matters with a stranger. Fortunately, this bias is on the wane. We live in a complex world, shorn of many of the protections our hero no doubt enjoyed, such as religious convictions and a strong family structure. Accordingly, many men have nothing to cling to when caught up in the firestorm of divorce. Talking to a professional therapist or participating in a divorced men's group is not wimpish and can be very helpful.

I strongly believe that psychological counseling is not the lawyer's business. The lawyer can offer some examples from his personal experience, but he is not qualified to assist you in this area by training or inclination. His orientation is that of a fighter. Paying a lawyer at lawyer's rates to function as a therapist is an expensive and ineffective form of therapy.

I would suggest searching for a psychologist, psychiatrist, or a therapist with the same diligence you displayed in retaining a lawyer. There are any number of quacks out there with little oversight from any licensing authorities. Like any other profession, the majority of psychological practitioners are honorable, caring individuals, but others must be avoided like the plague.

A good therapist will help you identify the difficult issues that you'll encounter as a result of the breakup and, equally important, the therapist will aid you in confronting those areas of your marriage that may have contributed to the breakup. If you made mistakes the first time around, you must learn not to repeat them in the future.

One of the most emotional aspects of divorce is telling the children, and both you and your wife may want to consult a therapist about how to handle it. I suggest telling them as soon as possible after you and your wife have made the decision to separate. More than likely they already know something is going on. All the studies say that, if at all possible, both parents should be present for that initial interview. Be honest: If it's clear the marriage is over, don't hold out hopes that maybe Mommy and Daddy will get back together again.

The children should be reassured that you both love them and that they are not at fault in any way for the separation. Decide on an appropriate story as to why the two of you are breaking up and stick to that story. Don't burden the children with accusations of blame and subsequent "revelations" as to why Mommy was impossible to live with. The children should not be forced to take sides. You want them to grow up into responsible, normal adults carrying as little parental baggage as possible.

Men's Rights Groups

Many fathers' rights groups have formed throughout the country. Most of them are small in number and suffer a fairly high rate of turnover, which may reflect the level of "burnout" among those trying to deal with the emotional issues of child custody, visitation, and parental child support. The leading organizations, which are listed in the Appendix, are excellent—tightly focused and service-oriented. Fathers for Equal Rights, Inc. of Des Moines, Iowa, and the Joint Custody Association of California are two of the most prominent. A few words of caution are necessary, however.

Some groups are nothing more than scam operations. They're easy to spot—their hands are always out. Take the case of Alex, whose story could serve as a paradigm of how not to handle your divorce case. Alex, a construction worker who was barely literate, had the apparent good fortune of marrying the daughter of a wealthy New York family. His father-in-law owned a major corporation which boasted, among other things, a legal department of fifteen lawyers. When their marriage broke up, Alex's wife presented him with a separation agreement drawn up by Daddy's lawyers. Intimidated by Daddy's money and the phalanx of legal eagles, Alex signed a ridiculously oppressive agreement that effectively removed him from significant contact with his daughter, and made him pay for the privilege!

Overwhelmed, out of work, and friendless, Alex moved back to his home state to stay with his sister for a while and regroup. He contacted a local men's rights group which assured him that, for the modest fee of $900, they would show him how to win back a share of custody and reduce his support payments. The inevitable happened: armed with legal motion papers any lawyer would ridicule, Alex flew back to New York to appear in court and be summarily vanquished by a top legal team assembled by his former father-in-law.

Coincidentally, I had contacted the men's group while researching this book. When Alex hotly demanded of the group what was going to happen with his case, he was told, not to worry, "our lawyer in New York is handling your appeal"! I, of course, had never heard of Alex until the day he telephoned me to inquire how his case was proceeding!

As noted earlier, this group is the exception to the rule. Almost every group I have encountered has impressed me with their dedication and selflessness. However, scam artists who engage in the unauthorized practice of law do exist—be vigilant.

To sum up, you should anticipate undergoing great swings of emotion. One moment everything will seem to be proceeding normally and the next you will be wondering how exactly you came to ruin your life. How successful the outcome of your divorce will be depends largely on how well you can control your emotions. They can not only poison your relationship with spouse and children but also affect the very outcome of your case. This is because at some point in the process you (not just your lawyer) must be ready to negotiate and compromise on tough, hard issues dividing you and your wife. And no one can negotiate successfully out of emotion.

Chapter Checklist

1. Understand the reasons for your anger, and control that anger.
2. If you're overly emotional, select a good therapist.
3. Worry about yourself.

4. Acknowledge your guilt, admit your guilt, and move on.
5. If you move, seek appropriate living conditions.
6. When you tell the children, be honest with them.

CHAPTER 6

How to Negotiate

Many people, particularly men, believe they instinctively know how to negotiate. They pride themselves on their ability to drive a shrewd bargain.

In point of fact, most of us are rarely called upon to negotiate major issues. Haggling over the price of a car is very different from negotiating a contract—which is what a settlement agreement is. Negotiating a divorce is a complicated process (and growing ever more complicated given the increasing complexity of our financial lives) with consequences that can be felt for decades.

It is commonly stated that divorce leaves women at a lower standard of living while their husbands retain sufficient moneys to pursue a new life with a new wife and family. I encounter few of these men. For most men, divorce is a financial disaster. The amount of support they are compelled to pay often reduces them to near-poverty level. Unable to adequately support two families on one salary, they live for many years in a state of economic desperation. Because men are perpetually haunted by financial worries, their life spans are sometimes shortened by this stress; their epitaph that they were improvident fathers and husbands. These are high stakes for the man who is negotiating the financial terms and conditions of his divorce.

Everyone has heard the statement that divorce is a messy business. In part, what is meant is that the entire process is so saturated with emotion that the parties find it difficult to make reasoned judgments. Unfortunately, too, divorce is often a client's first experience with lawyers and the courts. If pressed, most husbands would admit to feeling apprehensive about the unknowns of the legal system, concerned about their new relationship with their children, and worried about financial obligations and living arrangements. These uncertainties are a hindrance to a man who needs to be calm and rational at the bargaining table.

The ability to negotiate coolly is not related to the level of education or place in society. Every lawyer I have represented in a divorce matter has proved to be a difficult client. When it is your money and your family that are on the line, it is very difficult to remain objective, whatever your profession.

I remember a couple, Arthur and Robin, who simply could not remove themselves from the squabbling that had characterized their marriage. One-upmanship was the order of the day. Their settlement discussions had escalated from fights about money into a full-fledged custody battle. I was soon convinced that they were simply fighting their old battles in a new forum. Every time Arthur attacked Robin for her profligate spending habits, she responded by castigating him for playing around with other women. They constantly opened old wounds no matter what issue was on the table. I felt that they had never resolved these old disputes and it was unlikely they were going to do so now.

Therefore, I placed on the table the following question: What does this issue—custody—have to do with the past and what does it have to do with the present? Arthur came to realize that some of Robin's money concerns were reasonable. For example, she had new expenses like tutoring their child and braces, which had not been contemplated in the original amount of money allocated for support. Arthur realized that he was automatically assuming that his wife's admitted lack of financial acumen was responsible for her complaints when she really was reacting to circumstances out of her control. Instead of yelling at her, Arthur agreed to a modest increase in support, while being careful to set limits on his contribution to "extra" expenses.

Remember the story of John in Chapter 3, the husband whose wife cleaned out his house while he was at work? The next time the parties met each other, they were both feeling very emotional. As with Arthur and Robin, however, I set out to remove emotions from the otherwise orderly process of property distribution. I told both parties that they could spend the next year litigating who was entitled to what (and sending my kids through college in the process) or they could agree between themselves who was entitled to what possession. Given the choice, the parties saw reason, and John soon saw much of his furniture returned without the need for expensive legal maneuvers.

Your Lawyer Is Your Shield

In the divorce process, you need a buffer. This is why I have devoted a significant portion of this book to selecting a lawyer you are comfortable with. Because divorce is an emotionally overwhelming experience, you must have great confidence in your attorney. He must act as your surrogate in the give and take of settlement discussions. Your attorney is your champion.

Because some of the issues to be explored will be extremely painful to both spouses, it is preferable to have the lawyers make the appropriate arguments and absorb the inevitable counterattacks. It is imperative, however, that you have both prepared and empowered your attornies. Make sure that your lawyer possesses all the facts necessary and pertinent to the negotiations.

Some people just shrug their shoulders and say, "I'm leaving it in the hands of my attorney. I'm certainly paying him enough." Mistake. You hired your lawyer because he could present your case skillfully and in the light most complimentary to you. You did not hire a magician. He cannot invent the facts, and he doesn't instinctively understand your philosophy of life. You must make these things clear to him.

In addition to providing him with all the facts, ascertain that you and your lawyer agree on all the issues to be negotiated in the case. You want a complete settlement, with no loose ends. When you walk away from the negotiating table or out of the courtroom, you are entitled to feel that you have put this part of your life behind you.

A good lawyer will suggest that, immediately upon his entrance into the case, you must cease direct communications with your wife. This advice is not offered to exacerbate the frayed tensions between the parties or to inflate his own self-importance. He is trying to protect you from yourself. Because you are probably emotional, your responses to your wife's moves might divulge your position during negotiation or, worse, let her know what leverage you plan on using.

If you want to talk to someone, talk to your lawyer. Impress upon him or her your priorities in the give-and-take process of bargaining. Negotiating a divorce agreement is not unlike negotiating a Teamsters contract or a city workers' contract. Labor lawyers negotiate hard and tough, but never to the point where the other side suffers loss of face, forcing them from the bargaining table. In other words, push the other side *to* but not *over* the edge.

Developing a Strategy

Your attorney must understand which items are most important to you and, similarly, which items you are prepared to compromise on. Above all, you must give your representative the latitude to negotiate *realistically*. You don't want a Pyrrhic victory. Do not complicate the process with emotional arguments about minor issues that usually prove self-destructive.

Many lawyers dislike divorce work because there are no clear winners or losers. A party "wins" a divorce by coming out ahead on the issues that count. Most people forget this general rule and, human nature being what it is, one spouse will always feel he is paying too much while the other complains she is not receiving enough to live on.

Try not to fall into this trap. Ask your lawyer questions, read as much as you can, and quiz friends who have gone through a divorce to determine what *the legal norm* is for divorce payments in your community. One community can differ greatly from another community as one state can contrast sharply with its neighbor. If you are the propertied spouse, you are going to pay something—the key is to find out what similarly situated men in your geographic area have paid in the past. Once you know that, you have discovered the standard of fairness in your community.

Your lawyer will be able to refine your discoveries. If you tell him that your co-worker Joe Smith, with nearly the same income and family setup, pays $250 a month in maintenance to his wife for three years, an experienced lawyer will be able to confirm or disavow that amount as being realistic. He should be able to apply your facts to this figure and tell you whether you should anticipate paying more or less.

The particular judge in your case may have a history of being friendly or unfriendly to fathers. Judges are human and they have certain prejudices in how they divide property, award spousal and child support, and determine custody issues. There are a great many factors involved and no one can predict the future with anything approaching mathematical accuracy, but early on in the case you should have a good idea as to what the likely awards are going to be. You need this information for your own peace of mind and so that you can begin planning for your future.

You and your lawyer must develop a credible bargaining position. If you have learned that other husbands similarly situated to yourself have paid $250 a month in spousal support, perhaps you can negotiate to pay only $200 a month. But don't waste a lot of time and money in seeking to save that $50. A "scorched earth" negotiating position, wherein you fight over every dime and every concession, makes for great conversation in your local pub, but may end up costing you dearly in the long run. To obtain maximum results, a competent general does not send men and guns in equal parts to every sector he defends; instead he picks and chooses the areas where he will direct his firepower. Your approach should be similar.

In order to obtain the best possible results in your negotiations with the other side, your lawyer must convince his counterpart that you and he are willing to go to trial if necessary. If your wife's attorney suspects that you are afraid to assume the expense of a trial or that your attorney is inexperienced in the courtroom, she will use this leverage to her advantage during settlement discussions.

Although every case is unique, I have noticed certain patterns in my years of practice. In distributing property acquired during marriage, you must determine your priorities and guess those of your wife. Since it is unlikely that you're going to end up with everything, before negotiations properly commence, you must decide such issues as: Do I want the house or the family business? Do I need cash and liquid assets right now? Can I afford a new car after the divorce?

While you are developing your list of priorities and thus your grand strategy, you must assume that your wife is doing exactly the same. To maintain the military analogy, never underestimate your opponent. You probably know your wife better than anyone else. What will be important to her? On what issues will she concede? Develop your strategy accordingly.

Watch for signs that tell you the other side is bluffing. Keep open lines of communication with family and friends. You may hear things that will reveal your wife's strengths and weaknesses. If you want to be clever, you can plant false stories that you know will get back to her. The CIA calls this tactic disinformation. It can work for you, too, if wisely done.

Remember that you know your wife better than anyone else involved in the case. I once represented a wealthy man whose wife seemed to live in her psychiatrist's office. They had three young children. During settlement discussions, my client refused to be responsible for payment of any psychiatric bills for the children. Even I was surprised by his unyielding posture, because he had been reasonably generous on other terms in the agreement. I acceded to his wishes and we refused to reimburse on psychiatric or therapist bills, although we did give a little more in another portion of the settlement agreement. My client's wisdom became apparent years later. It seems that his wife had placed the children under psychiatric care from the age of three onward! My client had known therapy was all-important to his wife and his foresight resulted in his saving tens of thousands of dollars.

Also watch out for crude attempts to shame you into capitulation. Your wife may say things like "The longer this goes on the more public it becomes" or "Think of the children." (She probably won't point out that your agreeing to a financially ruinous settlement hardly helps the children.)

By the way, crudity may be distasteful but it can work. I know of a case in which a woman had an affair with her minister. The brief affair had nothing to do with the eventual breakup of her marriage, and she did not wish to harm the minister's reputation. In the midst of some acrimonious settlement discussions, her husband sent her a box with just a Bible and a tabloid newspaper inside. The message was understood. Henceforth negotiations went the husband's way.

Where a settlement offer is made can be important. If I have a client who is willing to "trade" physical custody in return for lower support payments, I never make the offer in open court. This allows the other attorney the opportunity to contend in court that custody evidently was not important to my client, otherwise why the linkage to support? I always make the offer "off the record" in the hallway, so to speak, to avoid the grandstanding that can be damaging to my client's case.

Just because you are getting divorced, your wife's personality has not changed. If she was an overbearing, nitpicking shrew during your marriage, you can assume that she will act the same way during settlement discussions. If she is selfish and a chronic "victim," don't expect that now she will be concerned about the future welfare of you and the children.

Similarly, your personality is unlikely to change either. If your traditional response to her constant bickering was to quickly throw in the towel, you are likely to do the same now. It is vital that you communicate the peculiar psychology of your marriage to your lawyer so that he knows what to expect.

Marital and Separate Property

In the United States two general sets of rules apply to the division of marital property upon divorce. "Community property" states (Arizona, California, Idaho, Louisiana, Nevada, New Mexico, Texas, Washington, and Wisconsin) assume joint ownership of assets. Most states require "equitable distribution" of marital property, that is—the division of property is based upon principles of fairness or equity. (Mississippi remains the only state that still distributes property on the basis of whose name appears on the title to the asset.)

In every state, marital property is distinguished from separate property, which is generally described as:

1. Property that each spouse owned individually prior to marriage.
2. Property that each spouse acquired by individual gift, either before or during marriage.
3. Property that each spouse acquired by inheritance either before or during marriage.

Although it can be argued that in certain situations, separate property can be "transmuted" into marital property, by and large separate property remains each spouse's sole property and is not subject to being divided upon divorce.

It is prudent to keep in mind this distinction between "separate" and "marital" property. In order for a property to retain the classification of "separate," it should indeed be kept separate from any jointly owned property. For example, it may be unwise to place separate property in a joint savings account or in a joint investment. Consult your attorney or accountant for advice.

As noted earlier, some form of equitable distribution is used by the majority of states. Property is distributed equitably, not necessarily equally based upon certain considerations. New York State's list of considerations is typical:

- The income and property of each party at the time of the marriage and at the time of the commencement of the action.
- The need of the custodial parent to occupy or own the marital residence and to use or own its household effects.
- The loss of inheritance and pension rights upon dissolution of the marriage as of the date of dissolution.
- Any award of maintenance as it affects each of the parties.
- Any equitable claim to, interest in, or direct or indirect contribution made to the acquisition of marital property by the party not having title, including joint efforts for expenditures and contributions and services as a spouse, parent, wage earner, and homemaker, and to the career or the career potential of the other party.
- The liquid or nonliquid character of marital property.
- The probable future financial circumstances of each party.
- The impossibility or difficulty of evaluating any asset or any interest in a business, corporation, or profession, and the economic desirability of retaining said asset or interest intact and free from any claim by the other party.
- The tax consequences of each party.
- The wasteful dissipation of assets by either spouse.
- Any transfer or encumbrance made in contemplation of a matrimonial action without fair consideration.

How to "Trade"

All things being the same, I usually advise my clients to look to the future. Attempt to hold on to the items with future potential and value. Trade the items that have higher current value.

Typically, the wife wants to remain in the house. She has spent years making it a home and it provides a stable environment for the children. If she wants to keep the house and it is not necessary to sell it to raise money, trade her the house. Don't give it away—*trade* it. Put the highest possible valuation on the house and contents, and compel her to relinquish her right to something you deem significant.

As with all marital assets, if you are giving up an asset, whether for cash or other marital property, you want that asset to be valued as highly as possible. The higher the valuation, the more cash or other assets you will receive in connection with the division. Too many men arrive in my office for the first time and announce, "I've agreed that she's entitled to the house. We'll work out the rest of the stuff with the lawyers."

This is the wrong way to negotiate. Every concession should require a similar concession from the other side. Assuming that you are trading the residence to the wife, and she questions your valuation, suggest that both parties agree to have one appraiser value the real estate. Depending on your strategy, you may wish to hire a realtor as opposed to a fee appraiser. Fee appraisers are more expensive but they do a great deal of work for banks and, consequently, are quite conservative in their estimates. Realtors, on the other hand, are conditioned by their profession to give high valuations.

If the parties squabble over valuation and both sides hire their own appraiser, make sure that your appraiser has experience testifying in matrimonial cases. If the valuation portion of your case boils down to a question of which expert is more credible, your appraiser's ability to testify will be crucial.

With respect to vacation homes, as a general matter I am inclined to trade them to the other side. Often, seaside or country homes are purchased at premium prices, and do not appreciate greatly in value. Let your former spouse worry about the mortgage, the real estate taxes, the homeowner's insurance, maintenance and association fees. Try to simplify your life as much as possible.

The Family Business

An entire book could be devoted to the single issue of family businesses and their valuation and distribution in divorce cases. It's quite likely that you don't want to retain your ex-wife as a partner in the family business (there is no surer way of destroying a business), so give her the house and perhaps something extra to buy out her interest in the business.

This is where your lawyer proves himself. Family businesses are notoriously difficult to evaluate or appraise. Try to keep it that way. Give your wife a note for the smallest possible amount. (After all, you have just given her the family home!) If it's a good business, it will provide income far into the future and will grow in value. A house will never appreciate in value at the rate of a thriving business. Therefore, a cardinal rule of any strategy should be to get your spouse out of the business that generates income.

If your spouse insists on staying in the business (if only out of spite), offer her a minority stock interest, especially if there exists a third partner or a shareholder who is loyal to you. If your wife accepts this offer, you have saved yourself the cost of buying her out, either by cash or offset of other marital property. At the same time, her minority interest will be weak because she will have no influence on the operation of the company with the other partner in your corner. As time goes on, she may grow unhappy and you can buy her out at a price much lower than contemplated in the marital settlement.

I have represented many successful businessmen who were surprised to learn that a business can be considered a marital asset. It certainly is such and will be valued just like the house and furniture. When I mention this to a husband, he often replies complacently, "There's nothing there to divvy up. Between you and me, my company is doing okay but the court is never going to realize that. My industry is so depressed that I couldn't sell the business if I tried."

Unfortunately, this rationale offers little protection. The value the law places on a business is not the book value; it's the fair market value. Even if no one wants to buy your business, an accountant can and will place a theoretical fair market value on it. Thus, if the accountant says your business is worth $500,000 and it is otherwise established that your wife is entitled to 50 percent of your assets, you are going to have to come up with $250,000 to pay her. The value of the marital residence may not be sufficient to offset that number. If you're cash poor, the court could care less. The court will make you sell some assets or put a lien on your remaining assets and make sure you pay the amount over the years.

A business in which you are a partner is extremely vulnerable. If your wife's attorney is competent (and you should assume she is), she very likely will seek to inspect the partnership's financial records in order to evaluate your share in the enterprise. There are ways of limiting this kind of inquiry, but the court will generally allow disclosure of the partnership's finances. As your wife's attorney knows, this investigation will upset your partners and therefore make you much more receptive to her settlement offer.

When it comes to valuation of the business, the husband who continues to operate the business will want as low a value as possible. This way he can expect the court to award him a greater share of the remaining property. There are many ways of keeping the value of a business down. Invariably, the husband-owner will have the business pay as many of his personal expenses as possible—

for example, meals and lodging, auto repair, gas, car insurance, medical and life insurance, computers, car phones, and such. These expenses will act to reduce the cash flow and, ultimately, the value of the business. At the same time, the husband takes a reduced salary from the business, which operates in his favor when the court calculates his support obligation.

The most favored method of undervaluing a business is "skimming," which is illegal. The owner pockets cash receipts and does not show same in the business's income. This practice is difficult to spot so long as the skimming is consistent. If a husband is already doing this, he should not accelerate his skimming on separation from his spouse because an accountant will pick up the change in income.

The beauty of skimming or playing games with business expenses is that the embittered spouse cannot now blow the whistle. To do so would invite IRS scrutiny of *both* parties' past tax returns and charges of tax fraud. If artfully done, a sophisticated owner can successfully undervalue his business. The wife's only recourse is to hire a good attorney and business expert, which will be expensive for her.

It's obvious that if you own a business and you have an opportunity to reach a settlement with your wife before her attorney brings in the accountants and appraisers, you should by all means do so. Accountants can only hurt you in this context.

If you retain operation of the business, even pending a final determination by the court, look at the business critically. Is everyone loyal to you? If not, get rid of those who aren't. If you suspect your accountant or bookkeeper of disloyalty, you have a problem; terminating them may drive their intimate knowledge of your business directly into your wife's possession. You are better off temporarily increasing their pay while removing them to a position where you can't be damaged. Be sure to change the locks, too.

If your wife actually runs the business and you have agreed to allow her to continue to run it pending final distribution of marital property, keep in mind that she has sole access to the family's largest source of income. If she continues to run the business, you are entitled to a monthly accounting of the receipts and expenditures of the business. In addition, see if she will agree to be responsible for all decreases in business income from the date you granted her sole operation. This will guard against her running the business down just to obtain a low valuation when all the assets are divided up later.

Alimony, Child Support, and Other Financial Settlements

Another crucial part of negotiation arises with the issue of alimony or maintenance. Alimony is deductible; child support is not. Consequently, attempt to style payments to your former spouse as spousal support rather than family support. Most important, think in terms of paying large amounts of alimony over a short period of time. Thanks to the women's movement, the law in most states now assumes that women can support themselves after a few years of rehabilitative maintenance. The days of women receiving large alimony payments for many years following the divorce are over.

Try to appear generous in your alimony offer. Remember, given the current state of the law, alimony has a short-term life. If you can strap yourself for a few years and make large alimony payments, your generous offer may lower the other side's guard and gain you concessions in other areas of property distribution.

How much you will eventually pay in child support is pretty well laid out in the statutory law of your state. You won't have much room to negotiate here, although most states permit parties to make their own support agreement, provided the children are not hurt and both sides have equal bargaining positions.

Other than statutorily mandated divisions such as child support, the remainder of the family assets is subject to negotiation. Essentially what happens is that all your assets are put in one marital pot and the haggling begins. The more there is in the marital pot the more there is to divide. Part of the strategy is to submit high appraisals for the assets likely to be awarded to your wife and light appraisals for the assets you will probably receive. If, for example, the marital pot is split 50/50, then you in effect will be receiving more than 50 percent of the true worth of the assets.

If your wife and her lawyer are not financially astute, there are many ways of splitting these assets to your advantage. If you have a large stock portfolio, you could divide the stock equally as respects face value but unequally in terms of liquidity. If you hold on to the blue chip, publicly traded stock, it will be easy for you to sell same, whereas if you give your wife restricted stock (stock that is restricted as to the dates on which it can be sold), she could have great difficulty unloading them. The same strategy applies to stock options. (An option is the right to purchase stock at a later date.) If you own the stock options, but are aware that they are going to decrease greatly in value in the coming year, trade them to your wife now while they have a high value. For example, say you own options are currently worth $300,000 but the president of your company told you privately that their value may decrease to $150,000 within two years. As part of your marital settlement, you should give the options to your wife in return for the deed to your home, which is worth $250,000 and will not plummet in value. Although you will appear to be making a concession, the reality is very much different.

Approach mutual funds, real estate investment trusts,

annuities, and bonds in the same fashion. Illiquid assets are more difficult to divide because liquidation usually carries a price. Also, they are more difficult to value. I typically advise my clients to trade away the headaches. For example, let us assume that you purchased some limited partnerships and, although they did well in the past, they're now starting to slip. You should trade them unless you need tax write-offs. Your wife may remember the times you bragged about how well the limited partnerships were doing.

The division of pension funds, IRAs, and deferred compensation plans is very common today. Almost every marriage includes some form of deferred compensation interest, and in middle-income families it can be the most valuable family asset. There are three usual methods of distribution: (1) a lump sum award based upon present value; (2) a future payout upon maturity of the pension interest; and (3) the pension interest is traded for something else in the marital pot. If the deferred compensation package is of any size, lawyers invariably retain accountants who are qualified to evaluate these assets. Today, failure to retain an accountant might be construed as malpractice.

To divide a pension, in most jurisdictions a court must issue an order that requires the plan administrator to "qualify" the order, that is, make sure the order meets the plan's requirements. My experience is that some lawyers are confused by the ever-changing pension field, and thus have a tendency to gloss over the subject or trade the pension away in favor of another more traditional (thereby more understandable) asset. Ask your lawyer if he knows how to draft a properly worded order.

Always Put It in Writing

Always put everything in writing. It's surprising how many people, sometimes even lawyers, will say, "Don't

worry about putting it in the agreement. It's probably unenforceable anyway. But I promise that I will ..." Another very bad idea, if you're the beneficiary of the alleged
promise. Make sure you spell out everything in writing.
There is no security in an oral agreement or guarantee. If
the oral assurance is meant to be kept, then why object to
putting it in writing? For the same reason, never sign an
agreement that contains blanks to be filled in later.

It may happen that you wish to insert a provision in the
agreement and the other side suggests that you are being
petty. Don't be intimidated. It's your agreement. If the
provision is legal and the other side agrees, put it in the
agreement if that is your wish. If you have a lawyer who
seems reluctant to take pressure from the other side, he
may grow testy with you for not agreeing to scale back on
your demands. Don't allow yourself to be pushed around.
You're the one who's going to have to live with the agreement.

When you get down to the final stages of formalizing
the settlement agreement and you believe you have
emerged better than earlier anticipated, ask that a clause
be inserted whereby each party agrees not to challenge or
appeal the divorce decree at a later date. This provision
may not be strictly enforceable, depending on your jurisdiction, but if your wife later tries to drag you back into
court, she and her lawyer will have to explain why they
agreed to include the provision. One simple paragraph
could save you a great deal of money down the road.

Sometimes when you are at the final settlement conference and the agreement is being hammered out paragraph
by paragraph, pressure will be placed upon you to sign the
document that day. If you feel you require more time to
study the document carefully, postpone signing for an additional day. Don't be intimidated by the fact that the lawyers understand everything so quickly. Remember, this is
their business. They do it every day.

If your lawyer wants you to sign something, don't be

afraid to ask questions—a common refrain of this book. Ignore this advice at your peril lest you suffer the fate of Dave. Dave lived in a state that required proof of grounds for divorce; that is, Dave and his wife couldn't simply allege irreconcilable differences and obtain a quick divorce. As the lawyers explained, one party had to agree to a fictitious act or two of wrongdoing to allow the other party to sue for divorce. It was all a fiction, they said. Not to worry. Dave saw no reason not to go along and agreed to represent that he had been "cruel and inhuman" to his wife on three occasions. The lawyers invented and wrote into the pleadings the three separate acts of cruelty. At first, all went well. Dave and his wife got their divorce and went their separate ways.

Later, however, Dave became concerned by the erratic behavior of his ex-wife. She was drinking heavily and had become abusive toward the children. Concerned for the safety of the children, Dave petitioned the court for custody. Then the other shoe dropped. The responsive pleadings to his petition quoted at length from the initial divorce papers wherein Dave had stated he was a cruel and inhuman person. He lost his custody case. Although he may be able to bring malpractice claim against his lawyer for advising him improperly, this hardly benefits his children.

Read everything you sign. Ask questions. Take nothing for granted.

Why Settle?

The ultimate question, of course, is: why should you settle? The simple answer is: you have gotten as much out of the negotiations as possible. A lot depends on your faith in your lawyer. You have been working closely with him for months. You have probably observed him in action with your wife's attorney and perhaps with the judge at a court conference or hearing on a motion. You have listened to his prior promises and assurances, and you have observed how they have played out in the course of negotiations. If you have faith in your lawyer, then accept his advice because that advice is crucial at this point. Before deciding to settle, ask him these questions:

1. Why is this settlement better than going to trial?
2. Are any parts of the settlement offer still negotiable?
3. Are there any additional guarantees that I can obtain?
4. What are the tax consequences? Is the amount of money I am paying reduced by income taxes?
5. Is this the complete settlement? Are any other items left outstanding to be negotiated later?
6. Do you have any reservations about this offer?
7. If we don't settle now, what kind of legal expenses can I expect if we go to trial?
8. What if we delay signing for a short while? Is it possible the other side might adjust their offer in our favor to deal with our hesitation?
9. Is this settlement fair or did I do better than I had a right to expect? If so, how?
10. If I don't accept this offer, will you continue to represent me in good faith?

As you can see, there are no conclusive answers to these questions. In the end, you will have to trust your gut and your lawyer's judgment.

The skills you have developed in negotiating your financial package will be sorely tested with respect to the topics discussed in the next chapter—custody and visitation.

Chapter Checklist

1. Learn the art of negotiation.
2. Use your attorney as an emotional buffer.
3. Provide your attorney with *all* the facts of your case.
4. Negotiate realistically, with an eye on the bottom line.
5. Develop a credible bargaining posture.
6. Be ready to go to trial.
7. Develop a list of priorities.
8. Negotiate for items with future earning potential and value.
9. Try to hold on to sole ownership of the family business.
10. Make sure all agreements are put in writing.
11. Don't be intimidated into settlement; however, a settlement should always be your goal.

CHAPTER 7

Custody and Visitation

No divorce issue is more problematic than deciding which parent obtains custody of the children. For the "hands-on" fathers of the 1990s, the issue has become doubly sensitive.

Whatever judges and commentators might say to the contrary, it remains very difficult for a father to win custody of his children, even when the mother is a marginal parent. In more than 90 percent of all custody cases, the mother is awarded physical custody of the minor children. Remember the movie *Kramer vs. Kramer?* Dustin Hoffman demonstrated that he was an extraordinary parent, particularly when contrasted with his wife who deserted her husband and child for eighteen months. Yet he lost the custody case! He only remained the custodial parent because of a magnanimous act on the part of his wife.

If he elects to contest custody, the father must understand from the outset that he is inviting a long, tough struggle against imposing odds. In custody battles, the father is *always* the plaintiff.

Child Kidnapping

Some men elect to circumvent the process by the underhanded tactic of absconding with the children to another jurisdiction. I always recommend against this tactic if only because it serves to exacerbate an already bad situation and because children can suffer severe psychological damage as a result. However, I have discovered that fathers intent on flight are not easily dissuaded.

Provided no court order exists mandating who has custody, in many states a parent has the legal right to take the children wherever he desires. Although it can be psychologically destructive to deprive children of their mother, the act of taking the children is not illegal in and of itself. By moving to another state (or even a country that traditionally favors father's rights), the father is forcing his spouse to expend financial resources to (1) locate her family and (2) contest custody in the jurisdiction of the father's choosing.

While the mother wages her struggle, years can pass. During that time the children may become more and more bonded with the father. Thus, when the mother finally wins a hearing on the merits, the father can truthfully argue that it is in the best interests of the children to remain with the parent to whom they are most attached. Some judges may not accept this reasoning but others will, particularly if expert testimony can be elicited to the same effect.

Launching a preemptive strike by removing the children to another jurisdiction is often successful, if only because the party left behind lacks the time and money necessary to contest custody in the new jurisdiction. If the spouse left behind is determined, however, he or she can wage a successful counterattack. All 50 states have adopted some form of the Uniform Child Custody Jurisdiction Act (UCCJA), which expressly provides that the newly adopted state lacks jurisdiction over custody if it can be shown that the absconding parent wrongfully brought the children to that state. Such proof might entail showing there was no emergency to warrant such flight or that the children had no prior connection with the new state.

If legal custody has been established, the Parental Kidnapping Prevention Act of 1981 (a federal law) prohibits the parent without custody from kidnapping the child. A government service helps track down the offending parent, returns children to the parent with legal custody, and punishes the offending parent.

In 1990 a Department of Justice study shocked the media but only confirmed what matrimonial lawyers had long suspected: that some 345,000 children are kidnapped each year *by a family member*, 80% of them by a parent. In contrast, only 200 to 300 children are kidnapped by strangers each year. Interestingly, a recent California study found that mothers are more likely to abduct their children *after* an adjudication, whereas fathers are likely to snatch and run *before* going to court. It's apparent that many fathers are pessimistic about their chances of obtaining a fair hearing on child custody, and are therefore driven to abduct their children. Because these abductions have become so widespread, perhaps the legislatures and the courts need to do a better job of enacting appropriate legislation.

If your child has been kidnapped, I suggest that you contact an excellent nonprofit organization, Child Find of America,* which provides free assistance in the return of parentally snatched children by helping to investigate and mediate between the fugitive parent and the child's legal

*Located in New Paltz, N.Y. (1-800-I-AM-LOST)

custodian. Child Find estimates that it has assisted in the location of more than 2,200 children in this country and overseas during the last decade.

Should You Fight for Custody?

Before you elect to fight a custody battle in the courts, ask yourself some fundamental questions: Can I handle the pressure of no-holds-barred, ugly litigation? Can my children?

In other words, it is vital that you undertake some serious self-examination. Remember: you are talking about the emotional well-being of your children. Too many parents use custody fights as a means of getting back at the spouse who wronged them. Your children's interests should be paramount. Put your anger aside for a moment and ask yourself: "Is my wife a good mother?" If your answer is yes, you and your family might be better off if you concentrate on obtaining liberal rights of visitation.

As a lawyer, I tell my male clients that they may dislike, even hate, their spouses. However, a woman who is a mother has a unique status: she is the mother of your children. Unless the mother is a danger to the children, it is in their best interest not to disrupt that relationship. To get back at a wife through the children is a pathetic and reprehensible tactic.

One husband whose case I handled cried in my office as he recalled his indirect involvement in the destruction of his daughter. After a particularly acrimonious divorce, he had won custody of his only daughter. He soon discovered that his new bachelor lifestyle—women, late nights, drug use—was beginning to have a deleterious effect on his daughter. He did the right thing and offered to return custody to his ex-wife, who was agreeable. Then the lawyers stepped in. His lawyer recommended that he not give up custody until such time as the mother honored other terms of the divorce decree where she was delinquent. Her lawyer had additional objections about his client immediately assuming custody. The end result was that while the parties, manipulated by their well-meaning attorneys, haggled over the terms of her return, the girl drifted further and further into a private world of despair. One day she killed herself. This may be an extreme case, but it does point up the terrible problems involved in custody battles.

Another factor to consider in deciding whether to try to gain custody is that you will be starting a new life. You will become more socially involved than in the past, and you will begin dating again. For this reason, it might be in your best interests to see the kids on weekends, rather than having them live with you. Whichever parent retains the bulk of custody will have a more difficult time in meeting a new potential mate. Sometimes by winning custody you win the battle but lose the war.

If you decide not to contest custody, don't magnanimously announce your decision prior to talking it over with your lawyer. Assuming the divorce promises to be contested, threatening a custody fight may win you concessions in other areas. You don't have to follow through on your threat, but if your wife is one to whom custody is all-important, by all means "blackmail" her. Threatening her link to her children may win you concessions in support payments or property distribution. You may feel guilty, but no one said the purpose of divorce was to make you feel good.

Take the case of Jerry. Jerry was an architect who one day walked away from a conventional lifestyle and, at the age of fifty, became a beach bum. As he put it, "I fell out of love with my wife and in love with the beach." They had two children. Unfortunately for my client, the judge in our case was famous for giving high alimony and child support awards. The last thing I wanted was to go to trial. Not only did the wife have a strong case of adultery against my client, but his general appearance invited raised eyebrows. In the course of discussing his case, I asked him if he wanted custody and was not surprised to receive an emphatic negative.

I hit upon the stratagem of having Jerry ask for custody anyway. I was counting on the fact that his wife would be unwilling to take any chance, no matter how slight, that she could lose her children to the new Jerry. That's how the case concluded. The divorce was settled by way of written agreement and not in open court, with the wife receiving custody together with very modest alimony and child support.

At times, a husband has little choice but to elect the litigation route. This often happens during an emotional separation, when women who have physical possession of the children try to hurt the husband by denying him access to his children. In these cases, there is really no choice but to immediately file a divorce action and seek temporary relief.

Some definitions are in order. Joint custody is an award of a child's legal custody to both parents. Having physical custody merely means that the child is living with you. Joint custody pertains to the right of both parents to make the major decisions concerning a child's education, religious training, health care, and such. Thus, if Mary has physical custody in addition to joint custody with John, this means the child lives with Mary but she must consult with John on all major decisions regarding the child.

Although more than half the states have enacted legislation permitting some form of joint custody, no law can make joint custody work. Only if the parents can agree to put aside their private quarrels, does joint custody stand a chance. Often, joint custody acts to the benefit of the father. The wife retains physical custody with all the attendant responsibilities. Meanwhile, the husband has the freedom to establish a new life, secure in the knowledge that every important decision pertaining to his children requires his consent.

Split custody usually refers to situations where the children live with one parent for a portion of the year and with the other parent the remainder of the year. Although this arrangement is uncommon because it forces children constantly to adjust to new environments, splitting is usually considered in cases where the parents live a substantial distance apart or when the children demand it.

How to Fight for Custody

Assume you have not been able to reach a custody settlement with your spouse and you remain convinced that she is an unfit mother.

As is constantly emphasized throughout this book, if you're forced to fight—fight to win. This means developing a successful, long-term strategy, which may demand the patience of Job and the cunning of Machiavelli. The strategy I suggest can be onerous to anyone save a father truly devoted to his children.

Most books and articles will tell you that the courts have replaced the "maternal presumption" by the test "the best interests of the child." Don't believe it. Most judges who entertain a new case are predisposed to grant custody to the wife. You can defeat the presumption, but you must do so by presenting clear and objective evidence to counter the maternal presumption.

Most custody battles are fought in the courtroom. Therefore, make sure that your lawyer is an experienced trial practitioner. He must be versed in the examination of witnesses and in marshaling evidence in a lucid manner. Laypersons are often unaware that many otherwise competent attorneys are not comfortable with litigation. Make sure that your attorney knows more than the address of the courthouse.

To win custody, you must develop a comprehensive strategy. Like a general preparing for war, you must assemble a detailed evidentiary trail that proves you are the superior custodian. Note well: your primary goal is not to destroy your wife's reputation. You can allow the evidence to infer that. Instead you must show the court why you are the better—indeed the inevitable—choice.

Preparation wins battles. If you and your wife are experiencing marital difficulties and you anticipate a contested divorce and a custody battle down the road, commence preparing your case long before you ask for a divorce. The aim is to gradually usurp your wife's role with the children in order to later prove that you are the principal nurturing parent. If she is indeed an unfit mother, this won't be difficult.

Also, in many marriages that are on the rocks, women "divorce" themselves from their families for a time in an effort to find themselves. The husband intent on winning custody can take advantage of this vacuum, by assuming many of his wife's domestic responsibilities under the guise of "freeing" her to pursue other interests.

Encourage your spouse to go to aerobics class while you stay home with the children or take them on an outing. Make sure that you arrange all the birthday parties; attend all the school conferences; ascertain that all the teachers know you as a concerned, involved parent; take the children to the doctor on your days off; drive them to all their athletic activities. Exclude your wife as much as possible. Encourage her disinterest if she is so disposed. If you're fortunate, the children will gradually look on you as their primary caretaker.

Learn to cook. Imagine the impact of the child's testimony in court that Daddy cooked a hot meal every night in addition to preparing breakfasts and school lunches. Ditto with respect to helping them with their homework and putting them to bed every night.

Timing is important. You cannot suddenly become a

super-father. The court will see through such transparent actions as giving the children expensive gifts and catering to their every whim. To win custody, you have to establish a history of caring for the children well in advance of the proceeding.

The judicial process demands evidence, that is, documents and other demonstrative material that prove the allegations you have made in your pleadings. Unsupported testimony is all very well, but hard evidence is precious.

There are many ways to generate evidence in a custody battle. When you take the children to the doctor, keep the receipts and cancelled checks showing your signature. Retain the receipts when you buy them clothes and books. Know all their teachers on a first-name basis. Other things you might do: Teach a Sunday School class. Coach the soccer team. Schedule periodic conferences with guidance counselors, special ed teachers, local sports officials.

Think of the impact in the courtroom when your attorney calls to the witness stand the family doctors, teachers, clergy, scoutmasters, and others. Further imagine their glowing tributes to your involvement as a concerned father and their damning inability to remember the children's mother.

Evidence works both ways. If you have a girlfriend (but want your children more), shelve her for the time being. Although dating while you are estranged hardly constitutes moral turpitude, you can never know how a judge is going to view the relationship.

When your lawyer presents your carefully accumulated evidence in court, he should do it in a constructive manner. I never try to destroy the mother on the stand. A beleaguered mother who is attacked by a smart-mouthed lawyer can easily garner sympathy, which obviously is not my intention. Instead, if she is unfit, I simply let the evidence speak for itself. If she forgot to pick up her first grader from school, I rarely ask, "Why?" (For all I know, she might have a good reason.) Similarly, I counsel fathers to testify factually, clearly, and free of hatred for the wife. The court assumes that you don't like your wife.

As is readily apparent, building your case in this fashion is not an easy task. It requires spending as much time as possible with your children. Since you are probably working, this means you must sacrifice every minute of your leisure time. You will find that this is an ongoing, exhausting endeavor. Don't make this choice lightly.

Courts become involved when one party (usually whoever has physical custody) files a motion for temporary custody or, in the Latin phrase, a motion *pendente lite*. This is an application to the court for interim relief pending the final decree. Typically, temporary motions address such issues as temporary alimony, child support, custody, and visitation. After hearing the temporary motion, the court enters the temporary order.

In addition to presenting the evidence previously described, it's likely that you'll introduce the testimony of a psychiatrist as an expert witness to evaluate your fitness as a father and the needs of the children. Concurrently, the court and your wife may select their own expert witnesses.

Approach retaining a psychiatrist the same way you did a lawyer. Don't leave this responsibility solely with your lawyer. Make sure that you are involved in interviewing the expert. Obviously, it is important that you both feel comfortable with the other. Find out if the expert has the qualifications necessary to impress a court (which is why you should always select a psychiatrist, who has medical credentials, over a psychologist) and whether this person is willing to say favorable things about you in court.

Our legal system is adversarial and combative. An expert must make a good appearance and must be able to withstand the rigors of cross-examination. The correct opinion, poorly expressed, can ruin your case.

Whenever the issue of custody arises, I am always asked, "Will the children have to testify in court?" It depends. If a child is mature enough to offer reliable testimony, a judge may allow her to give her testimony in open court or privately in his chambers (*in camera*). In either case, this can be traumatic to the child. After all, the child may feel that you are asking her to testify against one parent or the other. Such testimony can be very traumatic for a child and may leave permanent scars. This is an additional reason to think twice before commencing a custody fight.

Let us assume the custody trial is nearing an end. You have done a superb job in developing an evidentiary trail, your expert has been compelling, and your lawyer has awakened memories of Clarence Darrow.

Nevertheless, you should prepare yourself psychologically to lose. As I have already indicated, the maternal presumption is very powerful in custody cases. You can do everything right, but still run into a judge who cannot bring himself to take physical custody away from the mother. For this reason, you should seriously evaluate any settlement offers issued from the other side during a custody case. Custody disputes are long, expensive, and emotionally wearing not only on the children but also on the warring parents. If you have assembled a strong case, your spouse's lawyer undoubtedly will float a settlement offer. Treat this offer seriously. Sometimes obtaining very liberal visitation rights with other concessions can make legal and financial sense.

Be sure that your agreement is spelled out clearly in writing before you withdraw your motion. On the issue of joint custody, ask yourself if you will be able to work with your wife in the years ahead. Some people cannot even speak face to face, much less work together. If your answer is in the affirmative, spell out in the agreement every conceivable issue on which you, as joint custodian, would expect to be involved. Your lawyer's suggestions and any book of legal forms that contains sample clauses (your lawyer can lend you one) will help here. Don't be surprised to discover that your expectations differ markedly from those of your wife.

Visitation

Make sure that the visitation schedule is very clearly spelled out. What holidays are included or excluded? What about birthdays and vacations? Bad agreements merely specify "reasonable visitation," which invites future litigation. Once the divorce is over, you may find that you and your wife disagree on what is meant by "reasonable visitation." You must define the word "reasonable" by actually stating in the agreement when and where you will see your children. If you don't clarify this issue, you are asking for trouble down the line.

When you are negotiating a visitation schedule, always keep in mind the best interests of the children. It's not in their best interests to split a major holiday so that they're forced to spend part of it traveling between their parents' homes. You will also find that in the beginning the early visits with your children will be strained and artificial. This is natural. They probably don't truly understand what is going on and, in some cases, their perceptions are clouded by propaganda from an embittered mother. Although this will upset you, try not to contribute to their emotional turmoil by attempting to denigrate your wife.

I probably receive more complaints from men about visitation than any other aspect of divorce. Many of the complaints are more emotional than legal; that is, fathers usually find visitation periods awkward and difficult. To overcome this problem, I suggest that fathers feel free to communicate their unease to their children, provided they are old enough to understand. Visitation *is* artificial. Bring the subject out into the open. It will be better for all concerned to admit (to borrow from an old joke) that there is an elephant in the living room.

Also, guard against the danger of neglecting your role as a father to become a pal of your kids. Again, this is a common phenomenon. You will be seeing less of your children than you are accustomed to, and when you do see them, you'll want them to like you. (And it won't disturb you if they return to their mother with glowing testimonials concerning Dad.) You must resist this temptation. Your children want and need a father. Act like one.

Keep your life as normal as possible. When the children are with you for an extended period of time, don't automatically think in terms of vacation. It's important for them to see you in your normal everyday role and to see how you earn a living. You are setting an example of how an adult male conducts himself in society. These lessons are vital.

Treat your wife as you would like her to treat you. If she is anticipating your picking up the children, give her plenty of notice as to any change in plans. Try to speak with your wife directly rather than sending information through the children. If you have the children for dinner and they're young, schedule dinner sufficiently early so that they return home at their normal bedtime. Otherwise, their mother is going to have a difficult time with tired children the next morning. If you planned to take your son to a ball game, but he has a lot of homework that night, let him do his homework. In other words, his schedule should take precedence over yours.

When the children get older, their lives will become more involved. This is an inevitable and necessary socialization process. Don't be resentful if their plans run afoul of yours. In addition, if they don't wish to partake in some activity that you have selected, don't automatically assume that their mother has put them up to it. In fact, never criticize their mother in their presence. They will eventually figure out your motives, and you will be the one who loses.

Keep to a minimum the number of times that you fail to

pick up your kids. Nothing can be more hurtful to a child than to eagerly await a father's appearance only for the father not to show. It doesn't help if the mother is crowing with "I told you so's" in the background.

If your former spouse discourages visitation, try to reason with her. This is often difficult because a woman who discourages a child's relationship with his or her father is frequently a neurotic individual bent on redressing old grievances. If she insists on using the child as a pawn, try to make her see that she is only hurting the child. If reason doesn't prevail, don't resort to petty retribution by, for example, withholding child support payments. If you do that, you're helping to prove your former spouse's case against you with the child.

The case of Herb is to the point. Herb, a car salesman in New York City, married a woman from the South, and they had a son together. One day he came home from work to find wife and son gone, together with $40,000 from their joint savings account. Herb hired an investigator who located his wife in Georgia. After many threats and prolonged negotiation, she agreed to return to the marital residence. Five months later, she vanished again with their son and more money. Once again, Herb was forced to pay a lawyer and an investigator to get his family back.

His wife had no sooner returned the second time when she herself hired a lawyer (with Herb's money) who obtained a temporary order awarding custody to the mother, as well as child support and alimony. In addition, the court order barred Herb from the house! When he tried to visit his son within the guidelines established in the court order, his wife simply refused to answer the door. Out of desperation and anger, Herb started withholding support payments. Then he lost his job and became unable to make current payments. The court knew how to deal with this situation: he was thrown in jail for two days!

Herb now makes his payments on time, but sees his son, who resides in Alabama, only once a year. Even then he does not see his son alone but only in the company of his wife's boyfriend.

The moral of the story is not to take a chance with missing support payments. Instead, take your former spouse to court. It will cost you some money, but at least a court will set specific visitation times that must be honored. Your motion papers should include a request for recovery of your expenses and attorney fees, together with a request that such expenses will be automatically assessed in the future. Failure by your wife to comply with the court decree will allow you to cite her for contempt. Judges dislike parties who flout their orders.

Visitation can also become a problem when a parent simply fails or refuses to see the child. Unfortunately, no court has the authority to compel visitation. In the unusual case where you have physical custody, and your wife is neglecting your child, I suggest the following tactic: make a motion in court that you are entitled to receive more child support from her based on the fact the child is spending more time in your care than was originally contemplated. Either you will obtain a court order granting you more support money or you will have indirectly forced your wife to see her child.

Child Abuse

The physical and sexual abuse of our children has become a widespread national problem. The reasons for the prominence of abuse in our society are outside the confines of this book; as a matrimonial practitioner, however, I see more and more husbands accused of this behavior. Sometimes the evidence indicates that the husband indeed is guilty. But in many other cases the allegations are false, and employed as a way of "nuking" the man. This despicable but powerful tactic is increasingly employed by vindictive mothers to deny their husbands custody. Ten years ago child abuse rarely surfaced as an issue in a custody dispute. Yet one study claims that today fully 30 percent of all custody cases in the United States involve allegations of sexual or physical abuse by the father.

When such abuse is alleged, a court will immediately modify the custody arrangement to protect the child from future abuse. The criminal authorities are also routinely involved. Given society's increasing concern with this issue, the man fears correctly that his reputation will be irrevocably destroyed. He is faced with the task of "disproving" a lie and proving his wife a liar. If a husband does not have a convincing alibi, the court, to protect the child, will order supervised visitation subject to a social worker's investigation. During this time, the father's visitation time with his child will be limited and constrained by the continual presence of a third party. Because his spouse will enjoy nearly complete custody during the period of investigation, he will be beset with fears as to what new lies are being fed to the child.

With the mother vying to prove that she is the "best" parent, your child may start to manipulate you once it becomes obvious that you will do anything to curry favor. A troubled child might confirm untrue charges of abuse in an effort to remain in the center of attention.

There is no easy way to mount a defense against these charges. I recommend that clients caught up in this quagmire try to be as unemotional and reasonable as possible. Histrionics and impassioned pleas of innocence, however truthfully inspired, can hurt one's case, particularly when linked to a noncooperative attitude. The correct approach is to treat the allegations with disdain, and to demand an expeditious investigation. Consistent with the theme of this book, the father must take control of even this ugly portion of his matrimonial case.

At the initial hearing the father should request a psychological evaluation with a plea that the investigation be expedited because his limited contact with his child is hurting both him and the child. A medical examination will have already been performed on the child and the results must be demanded. If the investigation reveals that the father was an abuser or may have been an abuser, an immediate demand for a trial must be made. Medical and psychological experts must be produced to refute the investigators' conclusions. The expense involved will be onerous, but, given the gravity of the charges, a father has little choice.

Assuming you win at trial, you will petition the court not only for custody of your child but also very limited visitation for the mother. The argument is straightforward: if this woman would stoop to trying to influence her child in such a despicable way, is it not in the child's best interest to curtail the relationship while the mother obtains psychological counseling? In addition to requesting recovery of all costs, attorney's fees, experts' fees, and such, that you sustained, ask your lawyer to file a lawsuit for abuse of process against your spouse.

In the next chapter we move from negotiating custody and visitation to negotiating alimony and support. The issues involved are not as emotional, but failure to develop a realistic payment schedule can have very grave consequences.

Chapter Checklist

1. You win custody by *proving* that *you* are the fittest parent.
2. Think long and hard before commencing a custody fight.

3. Interview expert witnesses as you would a lawyer.
4. Define precisely the parameters of visitation.
5. Prepare yourself for allegations of child abuse and react circumspectly and vigorously.

CHAPTER 8

Alimony, Support, and the Separation Agreement

Alimony

The purpose of alimony (maintenance) is spousal support. Formerly, alimony was money awarded to a spouse having economic need until the death of either party or the remarriage of the dependent spouse. Frequently, alimony resembled monetary reparations after a bloody marital war. Fred put it this way: "My wife worked as a journalist before we married. There is no doubt in my mind that she could have turned to freelance writing if she had wanted to, but she didn't. Now my kids are fourteen and twelve, and my wife only thirty-eight, but she won't consider working. She sits at home painting her toenails while I write the checks. It ends up that I am paying her not to work, as well as paying for the children, and their education in private schools."

Today, partly thanks to the feminist movement, alimony

is usually limited to a specific number of years. Most state laws now intend alimony to be rehabilitative in nature. The theory is that the dependent spouse is entitled to moneys to reeducate her to enter the work force. After that, she's on her own.

If your marriage was relatively short and your wife is young, you should expect to pay alimony for a few years or less. The longer the duration of the marriage, the more alimony you can expect to pay. If you have been married less than two years, it is highly unlikely that a court will award alimony.

The right to alimony is no longer the sole province of the wife. All states, in theory at least, consider both spouses to be equally eligible to receive alimony. Generally, alimony is paid in monthly installments, together with the child support payment. Alimony terminates upon the wife's death or remarriage or upon some other event already agreed upon. Note that alimony is not a division of marital property. This bears significant tax consequences, which I will treat later.

Push aside for the moment the various states' sometimes complicated definitions of alimony and you are left with certain basics. Alimony is predicated upon two things. First, the wife's needs. If your wife earns a reasonable living, in today's climate she will have difficulty in getting alimony. Conversely, if she has never worked, possesses no marketable skills with little likelihood of obtaining employment, you may be looking at a hefty alimony award.

The second criterion relates to your wife's "prior standard of living" or, in the phrase beloved by the tabloids, "the lifestyle to which she has grown accustomed." In short, the judge will weigh your ability to pay. Be prepared for your wife to march into court with detailed accountings of what you both spent on household help, camps, vacations, country clubs, leisure items, jewelry, cars, clothing, etc. In response, you must argue that while your former spouse should live comfortably, there are limits. There is no compelling reason why she should continue to go on Caribbean cruises, simply because you both did so in the past. She's entitled to comfort, not luxury.

Ten years ago I would have given equal prominence to a third factor. It used to be that the degree of fault of the husband played a role in determining the amount of alimony awarded to his wife. Borrowing from the theory of punitive damages, courts were inclined to punish a husband for his misconduct. Today fault is no longer a major consideration in a judge's thinking, and alimony is seen simply as the husband's contribution for the needy wife's support. The state legislature would prefer that you continue to support your wife a while longer rather than have her become a charge on the public purse.

Can your alimony payments be changed at some future time? Certainly, if either party's circumstances change. Thus, if a husband loses his job, he can ask the court for a reduction in his payments. Similarly, a former wife who is suddenly faced with catastrophic medical bills may be able to convince a judge that she needs more money. Don't panic. The court won't simply hand her more money. She must prove a *significant* change in circumstances for a court to modify an existing agreement.

The mere fact that you begin to earn more money does not mean that your former spouse is entitled to any share of that increase. It is incumbent upon her to prove that her *needs* have increased.

Paying alimony is more advantageous than paying child support because the husband can deduct this type of support from his taxes and the wife must declare it as income. If you want to pay your wife a lump sum and get the alimony "nut" over with, or if you want to pay a fixed sum in monthly installments, speak to your accountant first. The IRS can classify this transaction as a distribution of property, in which case you lose the deduction. It follows that if you want to pay in installments, structure a plan under the guidance of a tax adviser.

Most agreements and divorce decrees provide that maintenance ends upon the death of either party or upon the remarriage of the recipient. Can you reduce or terminate alimony if your ex moves in with another man?

It's difficult. Interestingly, the double standard of society comes into play here. Although they're not supposed to, many judges will grant your wife a larger alimony award if she can insinuate you were an adulterous husband. But after the divorce, it suddenly becomes politically incorrect for you to point out she is living with another man out of wedlock, even if your children are witnesses to this living arrangement. In practical terms, you can only petition the court to reduce your maintenance payments if (1) you can prove that her liaison has been going on for a long period of time, (2) she represents herself as the boyfriend's spouse, and (3) it appears that she is being supported by him.

State laws differ on the extent of latitude you will be allowed in investigating a boyfriend's income. In some states income tax returns are privileged in support proceedings; other states permit such discovery. A new trend for individuals with resources is to enter into written agreements whereby the income and property of each member of the household are deemed the separate property of that member. These agreements can be difficult to set aside.

Also, if the boyfriend marries your former wife, he has the right not to testify against his wife. In conclusion, while you theoretically can consider the boyfriend's income in spousal disputes, the greater his income the more obstacles you will encounter.

In a recent California case, one man selected an unusual method of terminating his alimony payments. He entered a monastery! Since he had abandoned a lucrative job, his ex-wife missed her handsome alimony payments, and she took him to court. The court found that the man had literally acted in good faith by taking the vow of poverty, and this terminated his obligation to continue paying alimony.

A man whose limited funds prohibit the payment of both alimony and child support, sometimes finds it easier to avoid paying alimony as opposed to not paying child support. Because society is geared to pursuing delinquent fathers, if there's some compelling reason to be delinquent, it's advisable to pay the child support. The longer your ex delays in suing for her alimony arrears, the better your chance of avoiding this obligation. Simply put, a woman slow to react has to contend with the argument, "Well, if you need alimony to survive, how have you managed to live the last year?" By failing to pursue you immediately, she is demonstrating her lack of need for the money.

However, don't count on your wife not pursuing you for payment or, for that matter, her not receiving a sympathetic hearing from a judge. Because every debtor has a convincing story as to why he cannot pay his debts, many courts tend to ignore all excuses, even the honest ones.

Refusal to pay alimony is punishable by contempt—that is, you may go to jail. In addition, the creditor spouse possesses a whole array of remedies to pursue against you, including sequestration (having someone else manage your assets), income executions, and compelling you to post security for payment of future obligations. These remedies can embarrass you at your place of business. A wise man keeps this in mind when tempted to let his support payments fall in arrears.

Child Support

Child support is probably the most troublesome area of divorce law. It is a long-term financial commitment and it remains a difficult burden for most fathers. In New York, a father of an infant must pay 17 percent of what amounts to his *gross* income (basically only FICA is deducted). If he earned $30,000 per year, he would have to pay $425 a month in child support alone! $425 buys a lot of Pampers. But what seems to upset New York fathers more is that the law bases its calculations not on net income but gross income. (Some states deal in net income.)

Men experiencing the world of divorce for the first time encounter many surprises like this. Too often, the reaction is to avoid the stress of divorce by capitulation. They say, "Give her everything she wants. I need this to be over with." But these men live to regret their succumbing to pressure. Because they cannot meet their financial obligations, they either end up in court or they simply disappear.

A far better approach at the beginning of a divorce is for a father to examine his financial situation objectively and to determine what is best for him and his children. A divorce decree is similar to a contract in that the words contained therein are controlling in future disputes. When two former spouses end up in court again, they each will have their own story to tell. Inevitably, both stories are diametrically opposed. Because the first thing a judge does is to look at the wording in the divorce decree, it is essential that every provision of the proposed decree be weighed very carefully.

Wording Your Agreement

Don't assume that because your lawyer drafted the divorce agreement it necessarily follows that the agreement is worded correctly. Too many legal agreements of all types are poorly drafted. You must study the proposed wording yourself. Ask questions. Do not be intimidated by the impatience of others at the table, including your attorney. If a particular clause does not make sense or requires a lengthy explanation by your lawyer, it may well prove to be the source of litigation in the future. This doesn't concern many lawyers—after all, this is how they make their living.

For example, I have seen support clauses which mandate that the husband will pay a certain amount "for the support of the children." What happens when one child reaches the age of majority? You might assume that you can stop paying child support for that child and thereby decrease the monthly amount paid to your former spouse. But you might be wrong. Your wife could counter that your attorney drew up the agreement, and you had every opportunity to specify support on a "per child" basis. Since you did not you are now out of luck. The end result is confusion, expense, and possible litigation, all because the agreement was not artfully drafted.

It is inevitable that, as far as your children are concerned, you will feel guilt that they are being denied a "perfect" upbringing with their natural parents. If you are the primary actor in pushing the divorce, you will feel even greater guilt. A clever attorney for your wife will play upon your angst to obtain greater concessions, particularly in child support.

Do not allow yourself to be manipulated in this fashion. While you definitely have an obligation to support your children, the other side's demands may well be unfair. When you try to select a compromise figure, think in terms of how you would handle expenses were you still in the house. For example, it's desirable to pay for your child's dental work, but does she really need braces at this age? Is it necessary to pay for having her nose straightened simply because you feel guilty? Must she go away to camp every summer?

Unless money is no object, you must set limits. If your agreement simply states that you will honor all medical and dental expenses, you may end up paying for a lot of cosmetic work you otherwise would never have contemplated.

The Separation Agreement: Common Provisions

Visitation As noted earlier, a clause that is ubiquitous yet invites constant litigation states that the father is entitled to "reasonable visitation." To avoid this problem, spell out in the agreement exactly when you will see your kids. If you want them for six weeks in the summer and/or on spring vacation, make sure that appropriate language appears in the agreement. Consistent with reason, try not to leave anything to chance or the fertile imagination of your former spouse.

Agreements are a two-edged sword. Noncompliance on your part, for example, keeping the children longer than stipulated, will mean that you are in violation of the agreement. Repeated missteps of this type can result in losing one's visitation rights.

If the mother interferes with visitation, it's not advisable to retaliate by withholding the support payments. However, the law treats visitation and child support as separate issues. There is little doubt that women hold the upper hand here. What is a judge going to do with a mother who flouts your visitation rights? Put her in jail and thereby deprive the children of their mother? Unlikely. Your only hope is to keep bringing her into court in hopes an angered court will confer custody on you—but don't hold your breath.

Women's rights groups are loath to admit it, but the foregoing is the reason many men withhold child support. These men feel that withholding support is their only leverage against a spouse who is not playing fair. It is hard to prove them wrong. Instead of blindly blaming men, women's advocates should try analyzing these disputes dispassionately.

Grandparent Visitation If your wife doesn't like you anymore, her dislike may extend to your parents. It used to be that grandparents did not have a legal right of access with their grandchildren over the objection of a parent. This is changing, however. Many state legislatures and courts are concluding that such access is in the best interests of the children. If you anticipate this issue is going to be a problem down the road, try to insert favorable language in your divorce agreement.

Reducing Child Support It happens many times that the children are more often in the care of the father than was originally anticipated. If the agreement is silent on this issue, however, very few mothers are going to return a proportionate amount of child support payments or agree to a fair reduction. Therefore, make sure your attorney stipulates in your agreement that child support payments are eliminated during all periods your children spend with you, including vacations. Insert an additional clause that if in the future you are awarded custody of one or more of the children, the payments for their support automatically cease.

Income Tax Aspects of Child Support If you are supporting your children you are entitled to claim them as dependents on your federal income tax return. The separation agreement and the divorce decree should contain language to this effect. Sometimes both parents try to claim the children as dependents; the IRS will investigate both parents. (If the children have Social Security numbers, they use them to check for duplication.) You never, never want the IRS sniffing around your finances if you can avoid it.

Accounting of Support Money If you know your spouse to be a spendthrift, negotiate to have language included in the agreement to the effect that you are entitled to an accounting of how and where the support money is spent.

Escalator Clauses Many textbooks and self-professed "experts" recommend escalator clauses. They claim that if a couple inserts an automatic escalator clause that allows for equitable adjustments in the amount of alimony or child support, this in turn saves on litigation expenses and is a "fair" way of protecting the receiving spouse's interests. As a result, escalator clauses are becoming more common. I don't like them and I fight vigorously to keep them out of the agreements I negotiate on behalf of men.

There are two basic kinds of escalator clauses. The first is tied to an arbitrary index. Thus, if the consumer price index (CPI, which measures the rise in the cost of purchasing goods) goes up, the father's obligation increases proportionately. Note that the CPI does not compute the facts that a father may have lost his job or suffered a cut in pay. Yet the indexed escalator clause will require him to pay more.

The second kind of escalator clause is based upon actual raises in the man's income. These types of clauses usually provide that the father will automatically pay an additional percentage of his raise to the mother. Again, allow the real world to intrude for a moment. What if the father has remarried in the interim and has additional children to support? It's likely that he now has less money to distribute, not more. Although escalator clauses are touted as a "clean" way of avoiding future disputes, my experience leads me to differ.

Variable Support Clauses Variable support clauses are distinct from escalator clauses because they are intended to cover situations where the father's earnings are not stable. For example, a landscaper's income differs dramatically from winter to summer. The variable clause requires that the father pay a certain percentage of his income rather than the stipulated dollar amount. I feel this is fair, but some claim it is unfair to the mother because she can never predict when she is going to receive money. Agreed, but if she had remained married to the landscaper, she would have lived with this uncertainty, correct?

If you opt for a percentage clause, define what is meant by "income." Rest assured that your wife and the child support enforcement agency will contend that the parties intended gross income as the basis. From your point of view it makes little sense to pay in before-tax dollars; therefore, ascertain that your agreement precisely defines income as net income.

You are not trying to gouge the mother. Every agreement, not just matrimonial ones, seeks equity between the parties. The result of a divorce should not be to enrich the wife while impoverishing the husband. An agreement that is crafted after vigorous debate stands a strong chance of meeting the test of time.

Paying Child Support Twice   Men often complain that their former spouses spend the child support money on themselves, neglecting to buy necessities for the children. A man in this plight in effect goes in his pocket twice to buy the necessary food and clothing for his children. Justifiably angry at paying double the amount of support, he may try to deduct the additional cost from his next child support check. This tactic is risky. Unless there is language in the agreement providing that food and clothing can be substituted for paying the dollar amount specified, a court probably will not grant the man a credit. If you feel their mother is neglecting your children, make a record of the neglect and go to court to wrest custody from her. In practical terms, it is your only alternative.

Never pay child support in advance. If you come into a financial windfall and wish to pay off your yearly support obligation in one fell swoop, remember you have no guarantee that the mother will not blow the wad at the racetrack, leaving the children still to be provided for.

If your former spouse owes you money but fails to pay you, you cannot offset the debt against the support payment. The law regards these as separate issues. If your ex defaults in paying you the money owed, your only remedy is to take her to court.

Proof of Payment It is imperative that you are able to prove in court that you have paid your child support. Payment receipts and good record keeping are essential. Therefore, never pay in cash. A money order receipt only proves that you purchased a money order, not that you actually made the child support payment. I recommend that all payments be made by personal check. The canceled check should specify that it is for "Child support: month of March." While the wording does not completely prove that the check was for child support (the memo could have been inserted later), it certainly shifts the burden of proof to the mother to show that the father did not make the child support payment.

Medical Insurance As everyone knows, medical insurance is prohibitively expensive. If your wife works, strive for a clause that provides that she is equally responsible for the children's health care. If the mother is the custodial parent, consider inserting a clause that makes you responsible for insurance but holds her responsible for payment of deductibles. This guards against the spiteful wife who, bent on revenge, takes the children on unnecessary visits to doctors.

Attempt to limit or eliminate contractual responsibility for extraordinary medical expenses. If you are responsible for paying the orthodontic or therapy bills, it's only fair that you should be involved in deciding what care work is necessary. Also keep in mind that just because your current employer picked up your family's medical insurance, it is not guaranteed that your next employer will be so generous. The high cost of medical insurance is of great concern to most companies these days, and employer medical coverage is becoming increasingly problematical.

Think and then think again before you automatically agree to sole responsibility for insurance coverage.

Sometimes, upon separation, a spiteful spouse will cancel the family's insurance coverage. This is very dangerous to the family for obvious reasons. It is also a waste of time because every court will routinely grant a request for reinstatement of coverage.

Life Insurance Almost every agreement I encounter states that the children are to be named as irrevocable beneficiaries on the father's life insurance. This is fine so far as it goes, but what assurance do you have that the funds will be properly expended in the best interests of your children? One way to remedy this problem is to stipulate that someone you trust will act as the administrator of your insurance estate.

While on the subject of death, I suggest pausing to reflect before agreeing to language in the agreement that requires your children to inherit your estate. There is no legal requirement that you must leave one cent to your children. This may sound cruel, but keep in mind that at times parents grow to dislike some or all of their children. Or a parent may like his children through a second marriage better. At the risk of being repetitious, read your agreement very carefully and try to use your imagination to anticipate how it can affect your future.

Education Frequently, the father accepts the financial obligations for his children's future educational expenses. Although the father's child support obligation ceases when the child becomes of legal age (usually eighteen years), he may be agreeing to underwrite an expense far more onerous than child support—college education. If you feel honor-bound to accept this responsibility, at least stipulate that your agreement to pay is limited by your means at that time. If your wife's attorney is clever, she will respond with the suggestion that your obligation be based upon your "ability to pay." No good. If you possess the skills or education for a good job, a court might construe that you have the "ability" to pay, although this would not necessarily mean that you have a job. Consequently, limit the obligation to your "means."

Day-Care Expenses If the mother works, someone else must care for the children in her absence. Increasingly, fathers agree to assume part or all of this expense. If you decide to accept this responsibility, ascertain that you have control over the costs. Otherwise, what is to stop the mother from obtaining the most expensive day care available or paying her relative or girlfriend some exorbitant amount? In addition, the agreement should state that the mother will provide an accounting of all expenses incurred.

Pensions Courts have great discretion in the awarding of pension benefits. In a case where the husband has a retirement plan and his spouse does not, the court can award the benefits only to the husband, divide the pension between the two parties, or reserve decision until the employee reaches retirement age.

The theory underlying division of retirement plans is that at least part of the benefits were earned during the course of the marriage and, consequently, are marital assets which should be shared with the other spouse. The difficulty in dividing this asset lies in determining the actual present value.

Most men are not thrilled to receive the entire pension plan while watching their wife receive offsetting property in the form of cash or other liquid assets. After all, there is no guarantee that he will live until retirement age to enjoy the pension or, for that matter, that he will be with the same employer. Consequently, the recommended strategy is to divide the pension at the present time or divide it when the husband retires. This again is another one of those negotiable issues, because the wife's attorney, if she is an astute matrimonial lawyer, will want her client to receive this money when the divorce is finalized.

Profit-Sharing Plans Profit-sharing plans and stock-option plans are also marital assets with accrued benefits subject to division. Like pensions, the trick lies in determining the value of such benefits.

Military and Federal Pensions Military retirement pensions and federal civil service benefits are generally subject to division upon divorce. However, military *disability* pay cannot be attacked. If you are retired from the military, your spouse can only get a share of your benefits if she can demonstrate the marriage had a duration of ten years or longer.

Vehicles Every car has a value which is usually determined by subtracting the amount owed on the car from its current fair market value. The resulting figure (the equity value) is a marital asset. If you want to keep the Porsche, your wife will be entitled to another marital asset(s) of equal value.

Professional Degrees At one time a newly licensed lawyer or doctor could divorce and owe his or her spouse nothing even though that spouse might have supported the new lawyer or doctor through school. Many states now say this was patently unfair, and they now will consider the value of a professional degree or license to be marital property. Particularly in this context, valuation is a difficult and hotly contested problem. Since this area of matrimonial law is evolving in every state of the union, make sure that your lawyer is thoroughly informed on all recent cases that might bear on your case.

Selected Tax Issues During the course of matrimonial negotiations, many tax issues surface. The following examples are illustrative of some that most often crop up in this context. The parties' respective tax obligations and understandings should be clearly set out in the agreement. (Unless your attorney is also a tax expert, have your accountant review this portion of the agreement.)

Assume Harry and Wilma are divorced on November 15, 1993. During 1993 they made mortgage payments, real estate tax payments, child care payments, and state income tax, all pursuant to a joint return. Who gets what deduction on the 1992 returns, which are separate returns? The answer depends on whether Harry and Wilma live in a community property state or in a non-community property state. In a community property state, their earnings are held in common and each party is entitled to one-half of the appropriate deduction. If they live in a non-community property state, it is as if they were a married couple filing separately. As to child care payments, following the divorce, only the custodial parent may claim the payment, even if both made payments.

Harry and Wilma will be divorced in 1993 and both file a joint request for an extension. Do they now have to file a joint return for that year? No. It is permissible to file separate individual income tax returns.

If Wilma accepts a Rolls-Royce as a part of the divorce settlement and later sells it, does she have to pay tax on that transaction? Certainly, in fact she pays a capital gains tax on the original cost!

What about the legal fees incurred by Harry and Wilma? Are they deductible? No way. Legal costs of divorce in the United States are in excess of $1 billion each year. Did you really think Uncle Sam was going to forgo his share?

Other commonly encountered tax facts include:

- A transfer of house ownership as part of a divorce settlement is tax-free. When the owner-spouse sells

the residence, however, he or she is subject to a capital gains tax based upon the *original* purchase price.
- The IRS does not consider child support as taxable income to the receiving parent and, similarly, it is not a tax deduction for the paying parent.

The preceding examples are illustrative and not exhaustive. The higher the parties' income the more complex the tax ramifications. In fact, in a divorce agreement being negotiated between wealthy individuals, a good deal of the negotiating relates to tax issues. In other words, the tax treatment of support payments and distribution awards can save or cost one a great deal of money.

To conclude, every provision of your separation agreement, whether involving the more prominent issues of alimony and child support payments, or determining who pays for the baby-sitter, requires intense scrutiny on your part. You and your attorney must go through every detail in advance, develop a comprehensive strategy and list of priorities, and prepare to negotiate each and every clause.

Always negotiate realistically. Squabbling over minor points will transform an uncontested divorce into a contested one, a more expensive process that is treated in the next chapter.

Chapter Checklist

1. Limit spouse's alimony award to your true standard of living.
2. Alimony awards will be modified only if a party can prove a significant change in circumstances.
3. To obtain tax benefits, try to pay child support under guise of spousal support.
4. Approach escalator clauses with caution.

5. Review the wording of all agreements yourself—don't rely solely on your lawyer.
6. Don't withhold support payments as means of obtaining leverage with an obstructive spouse.
7. Try to have language inserted in the agreement that requires your spouse to account for all moneys received by her.
8. Don't pay support in advance.
9. Keep detailed records of all your payments.

CHAPTER 9

The Discovery Stage

Good lawyers always try to resolve matrimonial disputes without having to resort to intense litigation and in order to avoid the expense and uncertainty of going to trial. At the outset of your case, if the issues dividing you and your spouse are basic and few in number, your lawyer should telephone his adversary and offer to informally exchange relevant information regarding the two clients. Because this information must be turned over at some point anyway, it saves time and money if both sides furnish it voluntarily.

Many times a case can be resolved on the basis of one or two meetings between the parties. Obviously, much depends on the cooperation between the parties and their lawyers, who one hopes are more interested in professionally representing their clients than in expensive grandstanding.

Don't expect your lawyer to lie for you. Attorneys take an oath and are officers of the court. Only a foolish attorney would risk his license to gain an edge for his client. Of course, if the other side fails to request certain information, through ignorance or lack of skill, your lawyer does not have to disclose all the information in his possession.

A pal may boast of his lawyer who was totally uncooperative with his wife's attorney. There is a difference between a zealous defense and noncooperation. The lawyer who is known among other lawyers for being unnecessarily obstructive will find that his reputation precedes him. He will be fought tooth and nail by his peers, and you will have the privilege of paying for these legal games if you retain him.

If your case promises to be adversarial, after the complaint is filed, both attorneys will undertake "discovery," in order to learn everything possible about the case. Through devices such as depositions, written interrogatories, and appraisals your lawyer will seek to "discover" the full extent of income and property held by your spouse, what evidence will be used as grounds for divorce, and the fitness of the other spouse as a parent.

Interrogatories are written questions prepared by an attorney which the other party must answer under oath and in writing. An interrogatory answer that differs from a response at trial will be used at trial to challenge the witness's veracity. Notices to produce demand documents and subpoenas require outsiders to provide documents and/or to testify on relevant matters.

These discovery tools usually "flesh out" bare-bones responses on net worth statements and the initial pleadings. For example, if your wife claims you were cruel toward her, a properly drafted interrogatory will force her to detail when and where you were allegedly cruel, how many times, who else was present, the circumstances, what was said, what physical acts are being alleged, and so on.

A deposition is an oral examination of a party under oath. Generally, the deposition is taken in the lawyer's office in the presence of a court reporter who takes down the questions and answers, later typing them into booklet form. Although the deposition is relatively informal, it is the closest thing to being on a witness stand and answering questions in court. A deposition can be an uncomfortable, even unnerving experience for an unprepared witness.

At trial, if you state a fact which is at variance from what you testified to at your deposition, the deposition can be used to discredit you. An example:

Q. "Mr. Sweeney, prior to the commencement of this lawsuit, did you own a safety deposit box?"

A. "Yes."

Q. "Mr. Sweeney, do you remember testifying at a deposition on November 12, 1992?"

A. "Yes."

Q. "And did you swear to tell the truth at that time?"

A. "Yes."

Q. "And after the deposition, were you given time to review the transcript of the deposition?"

A. "Yes."

Q. "And did you appear before a notary public and for a second time swear to the truth of those statements contained in the deposition?"

A. "Yes."

Q. "And were you asked this question and did you give this answer—Question: Did you own a safety deposit box prior to the time you began this action? And did you give this answer—Answer: No."

This witness has now been discredited. If artfully done, all of his trial testimony may now be suspect in the minds of the judge or jury. Your deposition is crucial to your case. If you prove to be an excellent witness, difficult to rattle or trap, your spouse's lawyer will think twice about going to trial.

In some cases, depositions serve the purpose of convincing a litigant that settlement might be preferable to going to trial. If a wife has exaggerated the misconduct of her husband in her complaint, the withering questions she will receive at the deposition may lead her to reconsider repeating the experience at trial.

In Martin's case, the very threat of a deposition proved effective. He was married to an utterly despicable woman. In the course of a twenty-year marriage, her bullying tactics had reduced him to the status of slave. His final and only act of rebellion was to flee his home and seek a divorce. But his wife was not deterred. In addition to marriage, Martin had made some big mistakes. He had falsified his tax return one year and had assisted a relative in obtaining an illegal abortion.

His wife's attorney, made aware of these mistakes, forced Martin to appear at a deposition to answer questions. The attorney knew that Martin would fear a potential prison sentence for one or more of his indiscretions, not to mention losing his job. Legally, these acts by themselves did not present a defense to the divorce action, but now the wife could contend that her bullying behavior toward her husband was provoked by his illegal and immoral activities. As she had so often in the past, she won out. Martin dropped his divorce action.

Lawyers have different styles. Some lawyers almost change personalities depending on what stage of the process they are engaged in. An attorney who has been a perfect gentleman in early meetings can become hostile, intimidating, or insulting during the deposition. Don't rise to the bait he is presenting. Remain calm and unemotional at all times.

During the deposition, or examination before trial as it is sometimes called, you must guard against testifying to something that is inaccurate or exaggerated. Make absolutely certain that you carefully listen to and understand each question before answering. If you're unsure, ask the lawyer to repeat the question or rephrase it aloud, and invite him to respond whether or not this is what he is trying to ask.

Answer only what is being asked. If you can respond by a simple "yes" or "no," by all means do so. Don't be afraid to say you don't know or don't recall. While you shouldn't avail yourself of amnesia too often, no one is expected to remember every detail.

Don't try to help the other attorney. It may sound amusing but through the years I have noticed that many witnesses have an innate desire to assist an examiner who is obviously laboring to ask a question correctly. I suppose it's akin to completing the thought of a stammerer. Resist this temptation! If your wife's attorney doesn't know her business, that's her problem, not yours.

If your state requires proof of marital misconduct, you will be asked questions that relate to any alleged misbehavior on your part. No one likes having their personal life probed by strangers. Don't let your emotions get in the way, however. And if a particular question offends you or gets close to a weakness in your case, don't betray your discomfort to your wife's attorney.

You do not have the right to refuse to answer a question unless your lawyer objects to the question and instructs you not to answer. Courts grant lawyers a great deal of latitude in conducting discovery, but your attorney should object if you are being asked the same question over and over again, only in different guise, or if the questioner is venturing into irrelevant territory. Often, your lawyer will object to the "form" of the question, but nevertheless then instruct you to answer the question. The reason for this seemingly contradictory behavior is that your attorney wants to preserve his objection for trial. If the judge rules that you should not have had to answer the question, the answer cannot be used at trial.

You must be silent during the deposition of your wife. If you constantly interrupt or make a general nuisance of yourself, the court stenographer will be making a record of your obstreperousness, which can only reflect badly on your cause. You simply must be prepared to hear uncomplimentary allegations about yourself (possibly including outright lies) because an embittered wife is going to love having the chance to attack you. Content yourself with the knowledge that you will have the same opportunity during your examination.

The timing of the deposition is all-important. Too many lawyers proceed in the manner they were taught in law school. Through written discovery they collect every last item of paper they can think of and only then do they move to depose the witness. Unfortunately, written discovery and resulting motions can take months, even years, before reaching some conclusion. Sometimes this means losing an advantage.

For example, a client of mine had not disclosed to his wife that he planned to seek custody of the children. He and I both knew that, once informed of his action, she would react with all the fury of a lioness whose cubs are endangered. Otherwise, she was not unfavorably disposed to her husband. Therefore, I moved at the beginning of the case to depose her immediately even though I was not in possession of as many documents as I would have liked.

As I anticipated, her testimony was not hostile toward my client and certainly not reflective of the vitriol she would have spewed later when she learned we were fighting for custody of the children.

The only documents that you will bring to the deposition will be those requested by the other attorney in his Notice of Deposition. Your lawyer may or may not object to certain of those documents. If your wife is seeking information concerning your finances, you can expect to bring your bank records for the last three years, savings books, wills, trust agreements, deeds, real estate closing statements, financial statements, insurance policies, and such. When I am hunting down the issue of finances, I always ask for bank loan applications and mortgage applications. Individuals have an understandable tendency to want to impress the loan officer as to the extent of their assets; if I'm representing the nonpropertied spouse I don't mind being impressed either.

After your deposition ask your lawyer to critique your performance. After all, this was probably your first experience of this kind of thing. A candid appraisal can help produce a much improved presentation of the same testimony in the courtroom.

I'm often asked, "Can I keep my wife from being present at my deposition?" Unfortunately, you cannot, because she is a party to the lawsuit. (The good news is your mother-in-law can be prevented from attending.) Similarly, you should attend your wife's examination. This way you will not be depending solely on your attorney's evaluation of the progression of your case. You want to get your own feeling for the strengths and weaknesses of both your wife's case and your own. And it will help you evaluate her as a witness. Your lawyer will appreciate your input.

If your wife has put your mental condition at issue by, for example, alleging that you have lost touch with reality or are a danger to the children, a court has the right to demand a psychiatric evaluation. Most fathers resent this intrusion, and you may be tempted to manipulate the questioner or resist what you perceive as his manipulations. I suggest that you not waste a lot of energy in trying to outsmart the court psychiatrist. They have been through this process a thousand times. They themselves and their tests are proof against attempts to mislead them. Try to answer their questions as truthfully as possible and let the chips fall where they may.

Don't try to paint a false picture of your marriage. Remember, you are in the middle of a divorce. I am reminded of the anecdote concerning Dame Sybil Thorndike. She and her husband, a fellow actor, had one of those storied blissful marriages. After his death she was asked about their famously happy marriage. "Did you ever contemplate divorce?" "Divorce?" she replied. "Never. But murder often!"

If you receive an unfavorable finding, don't worry unduly. In the world of experts, you can usually find one who, for a fee, will evaluate you in a favorable light. In the hands of a good lawyer, these contrary opinions can be disparaged in front of a judge and jury with the result that none of the experts will be believed.

Because court calendars and individuals' schedules are crowded, discovery can be a lengthy and frustrating process for the uninitiated. This is particularly true if one or both of the parties is venting spleen via outrageous discovery demands. Ineluctably, however, discovery will terminate in its natural conclusion: the trial.

Chapter Checklist

1. Prepare carefully and thoroughly for your deposition.
2. Never lie.
3. Learn the "rules" of discovery.

CHAPTER 10

Going to Trial

Going to trial is not for the timid. Trials are often expensive, exhausting, and laden with pitfalls. This is why so many trial lawyers are alcoholics or have their own marital problems. A full-blown matrimonial trial takes a toll on everyone involved—the judge, the lawyers, the jury, the children and, of course, the husband and wife.

Some believe that men have an advantage at trial over their spouses, given the fact that society encourages men to be competitive, and there is no more competitive arena than the courtroom. If this is true, the advantages should be exploited like any other edge. Winning at trial demands coolness under fire, steady nerves, and the ability to absorb and deliver punishment. My frequent use of military analogies in this book is not unintended.

Pretrial Considerations

Like most legal processes, a trial may seem confusing at first, but I hope the following explanation will shed light on many of the mysteries. In an earlier chapter, I emphasized the need to retain an attorney who not only is conversant with the intricacies of matrimonial law, but who also is experienced in trying cases. During discovery and depositions, you will have obtained a measure of your attorney's affinity for combat. If his or her abilities inspire confidence, count yourself fortunate.

Similarly, if you sense that your attorney is reluctant to try the case for reasons distinct from the relative strength of your cause, by all means ask, "Do you feel comfortable handling the trial or should I consider seeking other counsel?" If you conclude that he lacks confidence—sometimes the case with a young lawyer—you are better off knowing this before you walk into the courtroom, not after. If this occurs, ask him for referrals of other attorneys and follow the procedures outlined in Chapter 2.

Of course, just because your attorney is pessimistic about your case does not mean that he is not qualified to try the matter. If your lawyer recommends against proceeding to trial, listen carefully to his reasons. His experience and instincts are probably better honed than yours. He has examined the evidence and made judgments as to how effective you and your wife will be as witnesses at trial. In pretrial conference, the judge may even have offered his opinion of how he thinks the case will turn out. In the final analysis, though, the decision is yours.

In addition to considerable expense, count on devoting a good deal of your time to the trial. Although rumor has it that simple cases can be completed in a day, most cases seem to take many days, even weeks. The courts are overwhelmed, as are the judges, and frequent adjournments when the judge or the lawyers have other commitments are the rule rather than the exception.

For me one of the key ingredients in making this decision on whether to proceed or fold my tent relates to the presiding judge. Judges are human beings with the usual human prejudices. In private life, a judge can be amazingly down to earth. But our system of justice confers godlike powers on a judge the moment he or she enters the courtroom. This is why otherwise proud attorneys often become fervently obsequious when in the presence of a judge; His Honor possesses incredible power over the conduct of that lawyer's case.

Consequently, pay close attention to your judge both before and during the trial. How interested does he seem in the case? Does he appear to favor one attorney over the other? How friendly are the respective attorneys with the judge when court is not in session? They will never admit it, but some judges are pro-husband and others are inclined to favor a wife's cause. Some are liberal in granting visitation rights, whereas others may view frequent visitation as excessive and destabilizing to the child's routine.

The fairness of the court is integral to your case. If you do not find the judge completely acceptable, see if you can obtain a change of venue which will remove the case to another jurisdiction. You might even be able to have another judge substituted, but don't rely solely on your attorney to do this. More than likely, he will have to appear before this judge in other lawsuits. He will be loath to invite the judge's displeasure at being told he is not wanted. Therefore, you must exercise control over *your* case. If you feel the judge is a problem, let your lawyer know in no uncertain terms.

There may be times during the case when the judge will ask your opinion relative to issues that are in dispute. Or the judge may ask what you expect on the issues of custody and visitation. These exchanges are not uncommon. Some judges participate actively in the trial, asking questions of witnesses and others. Other judges restrain themselves and let the lawyers do the heavy work. If your judge is inclined to intervene and ask direct questions of the parties, prepare yourself in advance. Develop a short, succinct speech that covers your main concerns. Laypersons are often intimidated by the black robes and the unfamiliar setting of a courtroom. To guard against stammering incoherency or simple loss of memory, I suggest that my clients commit to memory a short speech, possibly with the aid of a mnemonic device. For example, a man concerned primarily with the issues of *c*ustody, *al*imony, *v*isitation, and keeping the *E*l Greco painting might keep the word "CAVE" in mind while speaking with the judge. In this manner, he can be sure he won't walk away from a dialogue with the judge having forgotten to raise a crucial issue.

A last piece of pretrial advice: Before the actual trial commences there are a number of court appearances where your presence is necessary, such as hearings on certain motions and settlement conferences. When scheduling these events, what typically happens is that the judge consults his court calendar, the attorney his appointment diary, and they both arrive at a mutually agreeable date. No one will ever ask you about *your* work schedule. If you complain, your lawyer will shrug and say it was the court's decision. Don't be intimidated. I suggest that you make very clear to your attorney what days you are absolutely unavailable for court appearances. This way your life will be less disrupted and the court process somewhat more palatable for you.

The Trial

A trial starts with opening statements. Both attorneys provide the judge with an oral synopsis of the case and how they intend to prove their case. A lawyer cannot make outrageous, unsupported statements in his opening. Each statement must be connected to the evidence that will be introduced during the trial.

The plaintiff then presents evidence in support of the complaint and the defendant presents evidence to refute the plaintiff's case. Trial procedure also allows for rebuttal testimony by each side to respond to new issues introduced by the opposite side.

Ultimately, of course, you will be called upon to testify on your own behalf. Your testimony can make or break your case. There is no disguising the fact that your appearance in court is indeed a performance. By this I mean you must present the facts of your case in a manner calculated to provoke understanding, perhaps even sympathy. If you're overly dramatic, you will receive the bad reviews that follow any ham actor.

Courtroom etiquette is indispensable to your case. Judges and juries (some states require jury trials on certain issues, such as whether grounds for divorce exist) obtain impressions based upon your demeanor and dress. Currently, there seems to be a regrettable tendency for people to appear in court dressed as if they planned to attend a softball game! Not only is this an insult to the court, it may hurt your case. Dress as you would for any important event. If your attorney doesn't make suggestions, ask him.

Never whisper in court; this upsets every judge who has ever presided over a court. If you have a question or point you wish to pose to your attorney, pass him a note. Never exchange insults or speak directly with your spouse. Don't playact. Too many people have a tendency to grimace or otherwise react to unfavorable testimony during the trial. Judges and juries see through this kind of behavior, so act as naturally as possible.

Don't lose your temper, which at times is easier said than done. A client of mine, a construction worker, went through life on a cash-only basis; he had never owned a credit card. Therefore, when he first split up with his wife, he made all his child support payments in cash. The inevitable occurred. In court her lawyer attacked him for not financially supporting his children, noting sarcastically that the husband had no canceled checks or receipts to prove his story. My client, who had a choleric temper, was enraged at the inference that he would neglect his children whom he adored. He suddenly erupted in court, calling his wife and her attorney "filthy ——— liars." Chaos ensued. His profanity and anger cost him the opportunity for an impartial hearing.

It's almost pro forma for women to allege somewhere in their pleadings that their spouse had an ungovernable temper, which resulted in mental or physical harm to her family. If you lose your temper in court you are lending credence to this allegation and perhaps to other allegations your wife has made. Therefore, never lose your cool. The wife's attorney wins by provoking you—don't give your case away.

Courtroom rules of evidence often impress clients as archaic and needlessly obstructive. Many times I have heard the entreaty, "Why can't I just get up there and tell my story without the lawyers objecting all the time and the judge refereeing on esoteric points only they seem to be interested in? It's as if I have to play in a game where only the umpires know the rules." This reaction is understandable. The rules governing courtroom testimony have evolved through centuries of trial and error. Western jurisprudence (like all human creations) is an imperfect system, but it remains astonishingly capable of ferreting out the truth. Part of the difficulty for laypeople lies in the fact that no one bothers to explain the rationales behind the rules. I will make a stab at remedying this deficiency in the following paragraphs.

Under the rules of evidence, you are only allowed to testify about matters concerning which you have firsthand knowledge. Thus, you can answer questions as to what you personally saw or heard. Your own opinions or interpretations are not relevant; that's why you're in court. The judge will make those interpretations. For example, if your wife rejected sexual relations for long periods during your marriage, you may testify to this fact, but you can't opine that she was interested in another man. Someone else will now draw or not draw that inference.

You can only testify as to personal observations. You cannot testify about statements someone else made, unless your spouse was present. This is hearsay. If your friend told you that he saw your wife kissing another man, your relating this conversation is hearsay and therefore not admissable. The reason for this rule is that your wife's attorney is denied the opportunity to cross-examine the alleged observer of this incident to determine its validity. Your friend must testify directly if you want this evidence offered to the court.

Not all judges adhere to the rules of evidence, especially during pretrial hearings. I once represented a husband who had a second job cleaning houses on weekends. Naturally, he had conveniently forgotten to tell me about this additional income. At the hearing on his wife's application for temporary support, her attorney produced a fistful of affidavits from satisfied customers, all stating how much they had paid my client. What to do? If the affidavits were allowed to stand, it would be tantamount to admitting to this additional income, thereby increasing the marital pot and the potential award to the wife. I jumped to my feet.

"I object to the introduction of these affidavits on the ground of hearsay, Your Honor. I am denied the opportunity to confront these witnesses."

"This is an informal hearing, counsel," the judge replied. "The rules of evidence don't apply."

"In that case, Your Honor, I request a ruling from the court to that effect and placed in the record of this hearing."

Because the judge did not want to admit in the official transcript that he was accepting hearsay evidence, he postponed consideration of the second income. Thus, when the wife received her temporary award that day it was based on a smaller pot than she had anticipated.

When your attorney takes you through your version of the events concerning your marriage in the "direct examination" phase of the case, he cannot "lead" you in your testimony. He cannot ask, "On June 1, 1990, did you see your wife punch your oldest child in the face and knock her down onto the kitchen floor?" You would answer "yes," but isn't it really your lawyer who is testifying and not you? Our legal system would prefer to hear your version in your own words, which is why leading questions in direct examination are forbidden. Thus, you should have been asked, "What, if anything, occurred between your wife and the children on June 1, 1990?" Obviously, you must be well prepared beforehand by your lawyer to assure that you know your cues and can give the expected answers.

Cross-examination by the other side's lawyer is different. Here the law assumes that the witness will be hostile to the questioner. Now the lawyer is permitted to ask, "Is it not a fact that you punched your oldest child, Julia, in the face and knocked her down to the kitchen floor?" The law assumes that the hostile witness will be reluctant to admit to damaging facts, and thus provides the cross-examiner with an additional inquisitorial tool.

After your direct testimony, your spouse's lawyer is entitled to cross-examine. For the witness, no matter how sophisticated otherwise, this is an unusual, discomfiting experience. In your direct examination you had the security of answering questions according to a script developed by you and your lawyer during hours of preparation. There is no script in cross-examination.

An experienced opposing lawyer will not simply take you through your direct testimony a second time. She knows that you're comfortable with your story and, above all, she doesn't want you to remain comfortable. Instead, she will attack only those areas where she senses weaknesses or inaccuracies. She may vary the tone of her questions from polite, to caustic, to downright hostile. Her mission is to make you stumble, to trap you into damaging admissions.

You will hear the lawyers objecting a lot during the trial. Sometimes a lawyer simply says, "I object, Judge" without further explanation, whereupon the judge overrules or grants the objection, again without explanation. This courtroom shorthand can be bewildering for the client. Again, however, the reasons for objecting are understandable, if the time is taken to explain them. First, an attorney may object to the *form* of a question as follows:

1. Leading. The rationale for this objection was covered earlier.
2. Compound question. A question such as, "Did you not close out your joint bank account on June 15, 1992, and soon thereafter commence an affair with your secretary?" is verbose, unwieldy, and likely to confuse the witness. Attorneys should ask only one question at a time.
3. Argumentative. "Do you mean to sit there and tell this court that you did not go on vacation to Bermuda?" This type of question is intended to persuade the judge, not elicit information. It is also inflammatory and forces the witness to be argumentative in return.
4. Lack of foundation. The court wants to hear the story from the witness's mouth. It is improper for a lawyer to suddenly ask, "Did you sell your AT&T stock to your best friend for one half its value?" The proper way to obtain this information is to ask whether the witness owned any stock, did he sell it to anyone, and for how much. This way the witness is testifying, not the lawyer, and the court has an op-

portunity to observe and judge the credibility of the witness.

5. Repetitive. A witness should not be forced to answer the same question over and over again. This rule also inhibits the clever cross-examiner who will ask the same question in a number of slightly different ways. A tired or bored witness will answer the slightly different questions with slightly different answers. In the end, the cross-examiner may be able to elicit discrepancies, thereby affecting the witness's overall credibility.

6. Presumption of facts not in evidence. Lawyers love to "load" their questions. "When did you stop beating your wife?" is a famous example and no doubt originated in some matrimonial case. Unless the beating is undisputed by both sides, the questioner is assuming a fact not in evidence, not to mention upsetting the witness (probably intended).

7. Irrelevant. To a lawyer, almost every question put to his client seems irrelevant. This is a fairly straightforward objection, however. You cannot introduce testimony or evidence that does not relate to the issues raised in the pleadings. Consequently, a husband may be a philanderer, but testimony to such effect is irrelevant if the only issue at trial is property distribution.

Before you answer a question, always keep one eye on your attorney to give him an opportunity to object. If he starts getting to his feet, delay your response until receiving direction from the judge.

I have gone into some detail in describing the bases for objections so that you might become a more informed witness. In addition, if you feel your lawyer is not objecting to certain lines of inquiry that appear objectionable to you, ask him why not during a recess. Remember, it's *your life* that is under scrutiny.

I also advise my clients that cross-examination does not always mean simply sitting there and absorbing punishment. Inexperienced attorneys will sometimes ask "why" you did something. This is known as "opening the door." While the rules of direct testimony might prevent you from bringing up certain issues, a "why" question can be responded to in almost any manner you deem fit. You might respond by using subjective or hearsay evidence that you would not have been allowed to introduce on direct. When the cross-examiner realizes what you're doing, she will start bleating like an apoplectic sheep, but the judge will smile and say, "You opened the door, counselor, let him respond to your question." I coach my clients to be on the alert for these opportunities. You go from being a passive goat staked out for the kill to a lion leaping for the jugular.

One last point on testifying. Be as concise as possible. Answer questions directly and truthfully but in *as few words as possible*. Never help the questioner! "Yes," "No," "I don't know," and "I don't remember" are perfectly acceptable answers. Most lawyers do not work with a list of questions written out beforehand. They have in mind certain areas which they want to explore and they count on using the flow of your answers to move the testimony forward. In other words, many lawyers make up the questions as they go along. The briefer your responses the less the questioner has to pick apart, and the harder you are making him work.

Once the trial starts, cases take on a life of their own. Don't be surprised if your lawyer departs from his prepared plan of defense. He may be reacting to the evidence that the other side is presenting and to the approach of the judge. You want your lawyer to be flexible, provided he keeps you fully informed.

As the trial unfolds, the issues and the amount of evidence available pro and con will suddenly become clearer. You and your lawyer will better understand the strengths and weaknesses of the respective cases. The same evaluation is going on with the judge and the opposing lawyer. Often, the judge will recommend that the parties adjourn the trial for a settlement conference. At this time, you and your advocate will have to consider once again whether it makes more sense to settle now or proceed.

I have found that trials are emotionally frustrating to some clients, especially those who are seeking justice, some kind of official imprimatur that they were not the bad guy. This is not the business of our courts, and I doubt it ever was. Today, a court is simply trying to sort out a fair verdict based on the law and the evidence presented. So, if you want the world to know your side of the story, you are going to be disappointed in the trial. Forget television with its premium upon drama and sensationalism. A good deal of court time is devoted to the dry recital of obvious testimony and facts and figures.

When the trial is finally over, don't expect an immediate verdict. Typically, the judge will take additional time to review the evidence and a decision will not be forthcoming for weeks, even months. The judge may then ask the respective attorneys to draft a judgment for his or her signature which will incorporate his ruling. As noted in an earlier section, some gamesmanship can go on here as both attorneys "interpret" the ruling. Professionals understand that the trial is over and reach a quick agreement on how the judgment should be awarded. It is then presented to the judge for his or her signature.

To appeal the verdict, you must ascertain that the issues you are decrying were in fact raised in the lower court. That is, you cannot suddenly bring up some new issues. If you did not bring up a certain argument when you had a chance, the law says you are out of luck. If you do file a Notice of Appeal, it must be filed within a certain period following the decision, usually thirty days. Appeals are very expensive (often costing thousands of dollars) and are rarely successful.

For the layperson, and even attorneys, litigation is a grueling process. Every intimate detail of a party's married life is suddenly bared for strangers to poke about in. In open court statements will be made and opinions offered that will not be easily forgotten. When the trial is finally over, the sudden rush of relief is usually short-lived. As will be seen in the concluding pages, the court's verdict doesn't necessarily mean the end of your case or your connection to spouse and family.

Chapter Checklist

1. Make sure your lawyer is capable of conducting a trial.
2. Analyze your judge.
3. Memorize a short speech incorporating the issues most vital to you.
4. See that your schedule is a factor in setting court appearances.
5. Your demeanor and dress are crucial to the presentation of your case.
6. Control your temper.
7. Observe courtroom etiquette.
8. Watch for opportunities to counter-punch during your cross-examination.

CHAPTER 11

Now What?

Once the divorce decree becomes final, many men are overwhelmed by depression. The feelings of shock and loss occasioned by divorce are not unlike the emotions experienced by returning war veterans. The analogy is an apposite one. Like the soldier, the divorced man may have been wounded (loss of family, income, home) and now society demands that he function normally in what has become an alien environment.

On the subject of divorced men and women, virtually every newspaper or magazine article focuses on the woman's plight. There are signs, though, that this unfair preoccupation is lessening. In a recent paper presented at the convention of the American Sociology Association, Walter Gove, a professor at Vanderbilt University, reported that it appears the psychological well-being of divorced males is worse than that of their female counterparts. This is not surprising given that divorced men have three to four times the mortality rate of their married peers. Men told

Gove that their divorces had caused them to question their sense of worth and competence. The study found that, by contrast, women appeared not to be troubled by such "symbolic" issues—their concerns were more pragmatic ones such as money or relocation.

In 1993 the National Center for Women and Retirement Research reported that women recover remarkably well from divorce. The study showed that women who had been divorced for an average of four years were happy, had a wide circle of female friends, had better times with their children than when married, and even obtained greater enjoyment from sex.

Sadly, many men are not up to the task of reconstructing their lives. They wrap themselves in a hard shell of bitterness directed at women, the legal system, and life itself. These emotions come to dominate their lives and poison all new relationships and experiences.

If you are one of these men, it is imperative that you seek help. It takes work to build a new life and you should know that many men have lived through experiences identical to yours. Some of them have formed men's self-help groups, and you can profit from their advice. A qualified therapist will help enormously, also. Above all, don't automatically reject the idea of counseling. You have never been through anything like this before and you are going to need all the help you can get.

Documents to Record

Completely aside from the issue of your mental and emotional health, certain concrete transitional steps must be addressed. As always, your lawyer will work with you, but it's important that you understand what needs to be done. Specifically, your lawyer will have to prepare certain documents, many of which must be recorded.

Real Estate: For real property, there will be new deeds, title insurance, leases, assignment of leases, assignment of homeowner's policies, and other documents.

Vehicles: It may be necessary to effectuate title assignments for automobiles, boats, planes, motorcycles, and other vehicles. Insurance coverage must be examined.

Personal Property: You should arrange a time and place to take possession of any personal property that has been awarded to you, such as jewelry, tools, household furnishings, and other personal effects.

Insurance: Modifying insurance coverage requires considerable paperwork. Your divorce decree may mandate that you carry life and disability insurance to guarantee your obligations such as child support and maintenance. Beneficiary designations may be changed. Health insurance may also require modifications. Pursuant to the divorce decree, you will have to conform beneficiary designations and furnish I.D. cards to beneficiaries. If your wife will be converting her previous medical coverage under your employer's policy to her own individual policy, you will have to furnish her with the necessary conversion forms.

Financial Instruments: Stock certificates and bonds may require assignments depending on the provisions of the decree.

Debts: The intent here is to sever the financial relationship with your spouse as cleanly as possible. Select a certain date and agree on the amount due from you and your wife on debts divided as of that date. Close all the joint charge accounts; change utility billing; notify in writing all prior creditors that you will no longer accept liability for the future debts of your wife. Typically, your mortgage is a joint debt—therefore change the mortgage and bond to conform to the terms of the decree. If a third party loaned you money in the past and your wife has agreed to assume the debt, obtain a release from that creditor. If you are assuming responsibility for a debt, get a hold-harmless and indemnification agreement from your spouse. If you and your spouse have agreed to an arrangement regarding mutual debts, exchange promissory notes. All this paperwork can be a major nuisance, but sensible precautions can save you a lot of future angst.

Bank Accounts: Change ownership title on savings accounts, checking accounts, certificates of deposit, money market accounts, and treasury bills and notes. Take a new look at these instruments with an eye toward obtaining a higher yield.

Income Tax: Discuss with your lawyer if you should be filing a separate or joint return, and how a refund or deficiency will be handled. Get written indemnification from your wife for any tax liability for past years. Review with your lawyer your tax liability for maintenance or periodic payments.

Your Will: Have your lawyer change your will to reflect your new status. If you have a large, complex estate, don't use your matrimonial lawyer for this task. Ask him to recommend an experienced estates attorney.

Trusts: Powers of attorney or appointment and assignments of beneficial interest may have to be effectuated for existing trusts. It's quite possible that you may have to consider new trust agreements to implement maintenance, child support, or educational needs as indicated in the decree.

Social Security: Note that the law was recently changed to permit a former spouse to collect benefits based upon the other spouse's earnings if the former spouse is at least sixty-two years old and was married for more than ten years. Under certain circumstances, a divorced wife is also entitled to survivor's benefits after the death of her former husband.

Just because you have obtained a divorce decree, don't assume that your legal involvement with your wife is over. Divorce agreements can be modified if either party sustains a change in circumstances. This is why some cases seem never to end (and one reason why many lawyers avoid matrimonial work).

The theory behind child support modification is reasonable. If the child suddenly requires more aid or there has been a substantial change in one party's ability to pay, many feel it is fair to modify a support order *in the best interests of the child.* In many jurisdictions, however, spousal support is also modifiable. In other words, you can make a new and successful life for yourself but have little protection against your ex-wife starting a court action to demand a greater share of your increased assets. Most states permit parties to stipulate in their divorce agreements that alimony payments must remain fixed, thus prohibiting a court from modifying the agreement at some later date. It is vital that your lawyer insert this protective clause in your agreement.

There is obvious need for reform in this area. More than ever before, divorcées are working women seeking and securing jobs formerly reserved for men. As women's incomes increase, it is only fair that the courts require a periodic review of this income in order that mothers assume more of the financial burden for the support of their children. Alimony and child support should not be punitive devices directed solely against men. Instead, the amount of their payments should be determined only by need and the ability to pay.

Child Support Enforcement

With respect to child support, the public image is that of the deadbeat father who fails to make his payments and thus deprives his family. This picture is so ingrained in our culture that to question it invites scorn.

Nevertheless, my experience dictates a very different conclusion. Yes, there are irresponsible fathers who deserve our opprobrium, but there are not as many as we are led to believe. As often happens, the truth is more complex. The problem I encounter again and again is that of men with limited financial resources forced to maintain two households. These men are not monsters; they are simply caught up in a system that refuses to assist them.

Where fathers are given a voice in the rearing of their children, delinquency of child support is much less of a problem. Studies conducted during the 1980s indicate a child support delinquency rate for joint custody situations of 6 to 8 percent (approximately equal to the unemployment rate) as compared with the 45 to 75 percent delinquency of child support occurring in traditional sole custody situations.

The real problem lies in the fact that too many women are unable to obtain employment at real wages in our society, and therefore are pushed below the poverty line. Instead of remedying the problem by providing good jobs for men and women in this country, society looks for scapegoats, thus placing blame on fathers who are unable to support two families. In addition, the government chooses to ignore the fact that a father can easily become unemployed for two or three months or longer, through no fault of his own. Is not that father entitled to a speedy modification of his support obligation? Why is it necessary for him to hire a lawyer to seek the modification? Where is he supposed to obtain the money to retain a lawyer when he is pleading poverty?

Some experts believe that it would be far more sensible for every state to enact a law mandating that child support obligations are to be based upon a percentage of income, thereby eliminating the need for support modification suits. If a father's income increased, his children would benefit. If his income decreased, his obligation would similarly decrease, and a greater burden would fall on the mother or the taxpayers.

Until the system changes, child support enforcement agencies will continue to harass fathers. Since it is easier for a wife to enforce an unreasonable award than for a father to modify it, these agencies are very powerful. At present they are collecting nationwide more than $4 billion a year. In many jurisdictions the Uniform Enforcement of Foreign Judgments Act allows a woman to contact the state branch of the Office of Child Support Enforcement, which in turn will track down the former husband. The primary enforcement mechanism employed is wage garnishment. Agencies can legally bypass the courts and go directly after a father's wages and other assets.

It is axiomatic that for garnishment to be successful, you must be earning a salary. If you are self-employed, however, a former wife may have trouble. If she has the resources to hire a lawyer, your life can get complicated. If you do not receive wages or salary, the lawyer can levy against other assets you own. Your former wife can sell off marital assets to pay for necessaries for herself and the children, notwithstanding that you had obtained an earlier restraining notice against such disposition. If you have a business and a big arrearage bill, the spouse can petition a court to appoint a receiver to seize your business or other income. She can even have you jailed for contempt.

Popular mythology to the contrary, courts are reluctant to jail men for failure to pay support. Since incarceration prevents a husband from earning money to pay the support, courts tend to use jailing as a threat to scare the husband enough to guarantee future payments. The remedy of civil contempt is tantamount to criminal sanctions, and the law requires a similar burden of proof to be met by the wife. She must establish *beyond a reasonable doubt* (not just by a preponderance of the evidence) that you intentionally disobeyed a valid, written court order and that you had the ability to comply with the order. Although some jurisdictions have shifted the burden of proof somewhat in favor of the woman, it remains difficult to jail a man who can mount a vigorous defense. A knowledgeable lawyer knows that a number of avenues of attack are available to him, including:

1. The order was not in writing.
2. His client lacks the ability to pay. (You're in trouble if the court finds out you are making other payments to the exclusion of your child support obligation.)
3. His client never knew about the order.
4. The order is being appealed in a separate proceeding.
5. His client never *intentionally* disobeyed the order.
6. The order is vague on its face.
7. The applicable statute of limitations has run.

Bankruptcy

The effect of declaring bankruptcy on their obligations is a favorite question of husbands. The answer is that bankruptcy does not discharge a husband from his court-ordered support obligations, but it will discharge his obligations with respect to other divisions of marital property. This is because federal bankruptcy laws have priority over state divorce laws.

Thus, in a settlement whereby the husband takes all the cash in return for his agreement to convey certain real property, in theory he could spend or hide the cash, declare bankruptcy, and allow the property to be applied to his debts. The ex-wife ends up minus the cash and property. Of course, a husband who deals fraudulently with the bankruptcy court runs the risk of having his bankruptcy petition dismissed.

Whether bankruptcy affects pension payments remains an open-ended issue, and the answer depends on where you live. Some courts have ruled that pension payment obligations can be discharged in bankruptcy. Other courts disagree and hold that such obligations survive bankruptcy. If this is a relevant issue in your case, consult your lawyer.

Time for Reform

Society has placed both spouses on a more equal footing under the new divorce laws. Because alimony and property awards are no longer gender-based, it is only fitting that every state should enact a law decreeing joint physical custody of the child. This would certainly be in "the best interests" of the child, because parents would be forced to redirect their energies from fighting to cooperating, from court battles to kitchen-table conferences. The child obtains two equal parents, both available, and both participating in the child's upbringing.

The Constitution regards a citizen's freedom of movement as sacrosanct. But what about a parent's right not to have his child made inaccessible? There is a need for legislative assurances that at least child support payments could be adjusted to compensate for costs of visitation, at the expense of the parent moving out of the jurisdiction. In addition, there should be a judicially enforceable agreement as to how visitation will be accomplished on a frequent and ongoing basis.

Visitation rights must be enforced more vigorously. It is axiomatic that a father denied access to his child will be inclined to withhold support payments as a means of leverage. If the various states applied as much diligence to protecting visitation as to the collecting of child support, the latter problem might lessen.

Support enforcement procedures have proved very effective against delinquent parents, but at the expense of due process. A man's right to be heard has been sacrificed to the desire to impose punishment. Society tolerates this suspension of rights because none of us favor parents who refuse to support their children. But what about the father who lost his job or suffers drastically diminished economic circumstances? The system must be revised to reflect changed circumstances before more fathers are condemned to a life of penury and flight.

Tax laws should be modified to provide dependency deductions for the support-paying parent, deduction of child support by the paying parent, and head-of-household status for the support-paying parent who must provide a residence for the child when alternate visitation takes place.

Although society pretends great interest in the child's welfare to rationalize its draconian enforcement administration, no agency bothers to verify that support payments are in fact used only for the child's needs. Our present system simply moves money from the pocket of one parent to the pocket of the other parent, all under the guise of child support. Support enforcement tools such as contempt citations, subpoenas, and investigations of records must be utilized to require the support-receiving parent to provide a verifiable accounting of support expenditures.

The sex of the parent should not be a consideration for

the equitable application of parent-locator files and parental kidnapping statutes.

America's divorce laws are based on a delicate balance between freedom and responsibility. These laws have survived for more than two centuries because, by and large, they have been responsive to the shifting sands of culture and opinion. Although women were once treated as mere chattels, that attitude has changed. Women are now legally entitled to a fair share of marital property. But it is imperative that in our haste to remedy old wrongs we do not deny men their birthright—equality under the law.

APPENDIX A

Glossary of Legal Terms

Action: A lawsuit.

Affidavit: A written statement of facts which is made under oath and which is signed before a notary public or officer of the court.

Agreement: An oral or written resolution of disputed issues.

Alimony: Support money paid to the spouse; also known as maintenance.

Allegation: A statement of facts in a pleading; the claim of one party against another.

Answer: A written response to charges made in the complaint.

Appeal: A legal proceeding in which the losing party requests a higher court to review the record and decision in the underlying case.

Appearance: The formal submission by a defendant to the jurisdiction of the court. It is customarily filed after receiving a summons.

Bill of Particulars: An informational document that adds information to the sometimes "bare" facts contained in the complaint.

Claim: A charge by one person against the other.

Community Property: All income and property acquired by spouses during their marriage, regardless of title, but excepting property acquired by inheritance or gift. Typically, equal division is the rule.

Complaint: The initial pleading in a lawsuit which sets forth the facts of the case, the allegations against the other spouse, and requests that the court grant a divorce or dissolution.

Contested Divorce: A divorce where one or more issues has not been settled prior to trial.

Count: A statement of facts in a pleading.

Counterclaim: A complaint filed by the defendant against the plaintiff.

Cross-examination: The questioning of a witness by the opposing party at trial or a deposition.

Custodial Parent: The parent with whom the child normally lives.

Decree: The final ruling in a case.

Default Order or Default Judgment: An order or judgment of a court which is based solely on the plaintiff's case because the defendant has failed to answer the allegations or make an appearance in the case.

Defendant: The person who defends against the lawsuit commenced by another.

Deposition: The testimony of a witness taken out of court under oath and reduced to a writing.

Discovery: Procedures followed by lawyers in order to determine the nature, scope, and credibility of the opposing party's claim.

Divorce: The final judgment that severs the marriage of two people and restores them to the status of single persons.

Domicile: The place where a person lives, and intends to return if he or she is temporarily absent.

Emancipation: The point at which a minor child becomes of age.

Equitable Division: A system of dividing property acquired by spouses in marriage which is based on a number of "equitable" or "fair" factors.

Evidence: Documents, testimony, or other material offered to prove or disprove the allegations contained in the pleadings.

Grounds for Divorce: The legal basis for a divorce.

Hearing: Any proceeding before a court where testimony is given or arguments heard.

Hold-Harmless: An agreement by which one person agrees to assume liability for an obligation and further agrees to protect the other party from any loss or expense based on that obligation.

Joint Custody: A form of custody of minor children wherein the parents share the responsibilities and major decision making relative to the child.

Joint Property: Property held in the name of more than one person.

Judgment: A ruling or order of a court on an issue in dispute.

Jurisdiction: The power vested in a court to rule in a case.

Legal Separation: A lawsuit for support while the spouses remain living separate and apart. No dissolution of the marriage takes place.

Lump-Sum Alimony: Spousal support in a single payment or in a fixed amount, paid in installments.

Maintenance: Same as alimony.

Marital Property: Generally, all income and property acquired by spouses during a marriage, except gifts and inheritances.

Motion: A written or oral request to the court for some particular relief, such as temporary support, more complete discovery, and such.

No-Fault Divorce: A form of divorce that may be granted without the necessity of proving one of the parties guilty of marital misconduct.

Order: The court's ruling on a particular matter before it.

Palimony: The payment of support by one lover to another, even though the parties were never married.

Personal Jurisdiction: The authority of a court to make orders regarding a particular thing and the power to enforce those orders.

Petition: A written application for a particular relief from the court. The term is often used interchangeably with "complaint."

Petitioner: Same as plaintiff.

Plaintiff: The party who files the lawsuit.

Pleading: Any formal written document filed with a court which requests some kind of relief.

Prayer: The portion of a pleading, typically at the end, which specifies the action the party is requesting the court to grant.

Relief: An order or judgment granting rights or assistance, etc.

Residence: The place where a person lives, sometimes the same as their domicile.

Separate Property: Property considered to be owned individually by one spouse and not subject to division.

Separation Agreement: A written agreement entered into by the parties which sets forth their agreements concerning property division, support, and custody.

Setoff: A debt of one spouse which is deducted by the court from the debt of the other spouse.

Settlement: The agreed resolution of disputed issues.

Settlement Agreement: The written version of a settlement which resolves certain issues.

Sole Custody: A form of child custody whereby one parent is given physical custody of the child plus the right to make all of the major decisions regarding the child's upbringing.

Split Custody: A form of child custody in which the actual time of physical custody is split between the parties.

Stipulation: An agreement between the parties or their counsel, usually relating to matters of procedure.

Subpoena: A document served upon a person not directly involved in a lawsuit, requiring that person to appear and give testimony at a deposition or a court hearing.

Summons: A document served upon the defendant in an action which notifies the defendant that an action has been filed against him or her and advises that he or she has a certain number of days in which to file an answer or a notice of appearance.

Temporary Motions: Applications to the court for interim relief pending the final decree of divorce.

Testimony: Statements made under oath by a witness in a court hearing or deposition.

Trial: A formal court hearing to determine disputed issues raised by the pleadings.

Uncontested Divorce: A divorce proceeding in which there is no dispute as to any of the legal issues involved.

Visitation: The right of a parent who does not have physical custody to visit the child.

APPENDIX

Fathers' Rights Organizations in the United States

American Divorce
Association for Men
1008 White Oak Street
Arlington Heights, Ill.
60005
(312) 870-1040

America's Society of
Separated and Divorced
Men
575 Keep Street
Elgin, Ill. 60120
(708) 695-2200

Fathers Are Forever
P.O. Box 4804
Panorama City, Calif.
91412
(818) 846-2219

Fathers for Equal Rights,
Inc.
3623 Douglas Avenue
Des Moines, Iowa 50310
(515) 277-8789

Joint Custody Association
10606 Wilkins Avenue
Los Angeles, Calif. 90024
(213) 475-5352

Men's Rights Association
17854 Lyons
Forest Lake, Minn. 55025
(612) 464-7887

National Organization for
Men
381 Park Avenue South
New York, N.Y. 10016
(212) 766-4030

State-by-State Summary of Residency Requirements and Divorce Grounds

Alabama

Residency—Plaintiff must be resident of state for 6 months prior to filing for divorce.

Legal Grounds—Adultery; living separate and apart for more than 2 years without support; imprisonment for more than 2 years; unnatural sexual behavior; alcoholism; drug abuse; confinement for incurable insanity for more than 5 years; wife pregnant by another at time of marriage without husband's knowledge or consent; physical abuse; lack of physical ability to consummate the marriage; irretrievable breakdown of marriage; voluntary separation for more than 1 year; incompatibility.

Alaska

Residency—No residency time limit specified.

Legal Grounds—Adultery; incompatibility; incurable mental illness and confinement for 18 months; drug abuse; failure to consummate marriage; willful desertion of more than 1 year; felony conviction; cruel and/or inhuman treatment; personal indignities; chronic drunkenness.

Arizona

Residency—One of the spouses must be resident for at least 90 days.

Legal Grounds—Irretrievable breakdown of marriage.

Arkansas

Residency—Spouse must be resident for 60 days.

Legal Grounds—Adultery; living separate and apart without cohabitation for 3 years; impotence; confinement for incurable insanity for 3 years; felony conviction; personal indignities; willful desertion for 1 year; cruel and inhuman treatment; drunkenness for 1 year; commission and/or conviction for infamous crime; nonsupport.

California

Residency—Filing spouse must be resident for 6 months.

Legal Grounds—Irreconcilable differences; incurable insanity.

Colorado

Residency—One spouse must be resident for 90 days.

Legal Grounds—Irretrievable breakdown of marriage.

Connecticut

Residency—One spouse must be resident for at least 1 year.

Legal Grounds—Adultery; life imprisonment; confinement for incurable insanity for total of 5 years; irretrievable breakdown of marriage; incompatibility and voluntary separation for period of 18 months with no prospect for reconciliation; willful desertion and nonsupport for 1 year; 7 years' absence; cruel and inhuman treatment; fraud; habitual drunkenness; commission and/or conviction for infamous crime involving a violation of conjugal duty and imprisonment for at least 1 year.

Delaware

Residency—One spouse must be resident for at least 6 months.

Legal Grounds—Separation caused by mental illness; irretrievable breakdown of marriage.

District of Columbia

Residency—One spouse must be resident for at least 6 months.

Legal Grounds—Mutual voluntary separation without cohabitation for 6 months; living separate and apart without cohabitation for 1 year.

Florida

Residency—One spouse must be resident for 6 months.

Legal Grounds—Mental incapacity for at least 3 years; irretrievable breakdown of marriage.

Georgia

Residency—Filing spouse must be resident for 6 months.

Legal Grounds—Irretrievable breakdown of marriage; impotence; adultery; imprisonment for more than 2 years for offense involving moral turpitude; alcoholism; drug addiction; confinement for incurable insanity; separation caused by mental illness; willful desertion; cruel and inhuman treatment; fraud; drunkenness; spouse lacked mental capacity to consent; incest.

Hawaii

Residency—Filing spouse must be resident for 3 months.

Legal Grounds—Irretrievable breakdown of marriage; living separate and apart without cohabitation for 2 years.

Idaho

Residency—Filing spouse must be resident for 6 weeks.

Legal Grounds—Adultery; insanity; felony conviction; willful desertion for 1 year; irreconcilable differences; living separate and apart without cohabitation for 5 years; cruelty; willful neglect for 1 year; drunkenness.

Illinois

Residency—Filing spouse must be resident for 90 days.

Legal Grounds—Irreconcilable differences; impotence; adultery; drunkenness; drug addiction; felony conviction; willful desertion for 1 year; cruel and inhuman treatment; attempted poisoning or other endangerment of life of spouse; infection of spouse with communicable disease; bigamy.

Indiana

Residency—One spouse must be resident for 6 months.

Legal Grounds—Impotence; felony conviction; insanity for 2 years; irretrievable breakdown of marriage.

Iowa

Residency—One spouse must be resident for 1 year, with exceptions for shorter time periods.

Legal Grounds—Irretrievable breakdown of marriage.

Kansas

Residency—One spouse must be resident for 60 days.

Legal Grounds—Incompatibility; failure to perform a marital duty or obligation; mental illness.

Kentucky

Residency—Filing spouse must be resident for 180 days.

Legal Grounds—Irretrievable breakdown of marriage.

Louisiana

Residency—Filing spouse must be resident for 12 months.

Legal Grounds—Mere desire to be divorced is sufficient.

Maine

Residency—Filing spouse must be resident for 6 months.

Legal Grounds—Nonsupport; cruelty; abuse; desertion for period of 3 years; insanity; alcoholism; drug addiction; adultery; impotence; irreconcilable marital differences.

Maryland

Residency—If grounds for divorce occurred within Maryland, no time requirement; otherwise 1 year.

Legal Grounds—Living separate and apart for 1 year; adultery; willful desertion for 1 year; insanity; felony conviction.

Massachusetts

Residency—If grounds for divorce occurred within Massachusetts, no time requirement; otherwise 1 year.

Legal Grounds—Irretrievable breakdown of marriage; impotence; imprisonment; adultery; alcoholism; drug addiction; desertion; cruel and inhuman treatment; nonsupport.

Michigan

Residency—One spouse must be resident for 180 days.

Legal Grounds—Irretrievable breakdown of marriage.

Minnesota

Residency—One spouse must be resident for 180 days.

Legal Grounds—Irrevocable breakdown of marriage.

Mississippi

Residency—One spouse must be resident for 6 months.

Legal Grounds—Irreconcilable differences; impotence; adultery; imprisonment; alcoholism; drug addiction; insanity; wife pregnant by another at time of marriage without husband's knowledge; willful desertion for 1 year; cruel and inhuman treatment; spouse lacked mental capacity to consent; incest.

Missouri

Residency—One spouse must be resident for 90 days.

Legal Grounds—Irretrievable breakdown of marriage.

Montana

Residency—One spouse must be resident for 90 days.

Legal Grounds—Irretrievable breakdown of marriage.

Nebraska

Residency—One spouse must be resident for 1 year.

Legal Grounds—Irretrievable breakdown of marriage.

Nevada

Residency—One spouse must be resident for 6 weeks.

Legal Grounds—Incompatibility; living separate and apart without cohabitation for 1 year; insanity.

New Hampshire

Residency—Filing spouse must be resident for 1 year or, if both spouses are residents, there is no time requirement.

Legal Grounds—Irreconcilable differences; impotence; adultery; cruel and inhuman treatment; imprisonment for more than 1 year; abandonment for more than 2 years; physical abuse; drunkenness; living separate and apart; mental abuse; when either spouse has joined a religious society which professes that the relationship of husband and wife is unlawful and refuses to cohabit with the other for a period of 6 consecutive months; when the wife of a citizen of New Hampshire leaves the state without her husband's consent and lives elsewhere for 10 consecutive years without returning to claim her marriage rights; when the wife lives in New Hampshire and her husband becomes the citizen of a foreign country without supporting the wife.

New Jersey

Residency—One spouse must be a resident for 1 year or, if the cause of action is adultery and said act took place in New Jersey, then no time limit.

Legal Grounds—Living separate and apart for 18 months; adultery; imprisonment for 18 months; unnatural sexual behavior; alcoholism; drug addiction; insanity; willful desertion for 1 year; cruel and inhuman treatment; separation for 2 years caused by confinement for mental illness.

New Mexico

Residency—One spouse must be resident for 6 months.

Legal Grounds—Incompatibility; adultery; abandonment; cruel and inhuman treatment.

New York

Residency—No residency time limit if both spouses reside in New York at time of filing and the grounds of divorce arose in New York. If only one spouse is resident at time of filing, the residency requirement is 2 years. Time period is reduced to 1 year if (1) spouses were married in New York and one party is still a resident; or (2) parties once resided in New York and one party remains a resident; or (3) the grounds for divorce arose in New York.

Legal Grounds—Adultery; abandonment for 1 year; imprisonment for 3 years; cruel and inhuman treatment; abandonment for 5 years; living separate and apart for 1 year pursuant to terms of written agreement which is signed, notarized, and filed in court.

North Carolina

Residency—One spouse must be resident for 6 months.

Legal Grounds—Living separate and apart for 1 year; insanity; incurable mental illness based upon examinations for 3 years.

North Dakota

Residency—Filing spouse must be resident for 6 months.

Legal Grounds—Adultery; insanity; felony conviction; cruel and inhuman treatment; willful desertion; willful neglect; drunkenness; irreconcilable differences.

Ohio

Residency—Filing spouse must be resident for 90 days.

Legal Grounds—Adultery; imprisonment; insanity; willful desertion for 1 year; incompatibility; living separate and apart for 1 year; cruel and inhuman treatment; bigamy; drunkenness; fraud; neglect.

Oklahoma

Residency—One spouse must be resident for 6 months.

Legal Grounds—Incompatibility; impotence; adultery; abandonment for 1 year; imprisonment; insanity; cruel and inhuman treatment; fraud; drunkenness; the wife was pregnant at time of marriage without knowledge of husband; gross neglect.

Oregon

Residency—If marriage was performed in Oregon, there is no residency requirement; otherwise 6 months.

Legal Grounds—Irreconcilable differences; fraud; minor married under age of legal consent; spouse lacked mental capacity to consent.

Pennsylvania

Residency—One spouse must be resident for 6 months.

Legal Grounds—Irretrievable breakdown of marriage; adultery; bigamy; imprisonment for 2 or more years; insanity; willful desertion for 1 year; cruel and inhuman treatment; personal indignities.

Rhode Island

Residency—One spouse must be resident for 1 year.

Legal Grounds—Irreconcilable differences; adultery; impotence; abandonment; alcoholism; drug addiction; insanity; failure to consummate marriage; willful desertion for 5 years or less in certain circumstances; cruel and inhuman treatment; bigamy; life imprisonment; spouse of unsound mind; incest; gross neglect.

South Carolina

Residency—If both spouses are residents, the requirement is 3 months; otherwise the filing spouse must be resident for 6 months.

Legal Grounds—Living separate and apart for 1 year; adultery; alcoholism; drug addiction; physical abuse; willful desertion for 1 year.

South Dakota

Residency—Filing spouse must be resident and remain resident until divorce is finalized.

Legal Grounds—Irreconcilable differences; adultery; insanity; felony conviction; willful desertion; cruel and inhuman treatment; willful neglect; drunkenness; separation caused by misconduct.

Tennessee

Residency—Filing spouse must be resident. If the grounds arose outside Tennessee and the plaintiff resided outside state, either spouse must have been a resident for 6 months prior to filing the divorce action.

Legal Grounds—Irreconcilable differences; adultery; impotence; felony conviction; alcoholism; drug addiction; wife pregnant at time of marriage without husband's knowledge; willful desertion for 1 year; bigamy; endangering the life of the spouse; commission and/or conviction of an infamous crime; refusing to locate to Tennessee with a spouse and willfully absenting oneself from the new residence for 2 years.

Texas

Residency—One spouse must be resident for 6 months.

Legal Grounds—Marriage has become insupportable due to marital discord; living separate and apart for 3 years; adultery; abandonment; insanity; felony conviction; cruel and inhuman treatment.

Utah

Residency—Filing spouse must be resident for 3 months.

Legal Grounds—Adultery; irreconcilable differences; impotence; willful neglect; living separate and apart for 3 years; felony conviction; cruel and inhuman treatment; willful neglect; insanity; drunkenness.

Vermont

Residency—One spouse must be resident for 6 months.

Legal Grounds—Living separate and apart for 6 consecutive months; adultery; imprisonment for 3 years; willful desertion for 7 years; cruel and inhuman treatment; insanity; gross neglect.

Virginia

Residency—One spouse must be resident for 6 months.

Legal Grounds—Adultery; abandonment; homosexual adultery; felony conviction; cruelty; willful desertion; living separate and apart for 1 year (or 6 months if no minor children and separation agreement exists).

Washington

Residency—Filing spouse must be resident; no time requirement.

Legal Grounds—Irretrievable breakdown of marriage.

West Virginia

Residency—If marriage was performed in state and one spouse is resident at time of filing, there is no durational time limit; otherwise one spouse must be resident for at least 1 year.

Legal Grounds—Irreconcilable differences; living separate and apart for 1 year; adultery; abandonment for 6 months; alcoholism; drug addiction; insanity; physical abuse; felony conviction; cruel and inhuman treatment; drunkenness; willful neglect of spouse or child.

Wisconsin

Residency—One spouse must be resident for 6 months.

Legal Grounds—Irretrievable breakdown of marriage.

Wyoming

Residency—Marriage must have been performed in Wyoming and filing spouse has resided in state continuously since date of marriage or filing spouse has been resident for 60 days.

Legal Grounds—Irreconcilable differences; insanity.

INDEX